Peggy McColl

On Being...

The Creator of Your Destiny

Peggy McColl

www.destinies.com

Destinies Publishing
1 Stafford Road, Suite 312
Nepean, Ontario K2H 1B9
(613) 299-5722

ISBN 0-9730431-0-5
Printed and bound in Canada

Editing by Janet Shorten
Illustrations by Fernando Martinez, 3dA Multimedia Inc.

Production by Baird O'Keefe Publishing Inc., *Publication Specialists*
        Wendelina O'Keefe, Designer
        Gail Baird, Managing Editor
        Cover photo © PhotoDisc Inc.

Printing number 10 9 8 7 6 5 4 3 2 1

National Library of Canada Cataloguing in Publication Data

McColl, Peggy
        On being... the creator of your destiny

Includes bibliographical references.
ISBN 0-9730431-0-5

    1. Self-actualization (Psychology) I. Title.

BF637.S4M18 2002   158.1   C2002-900685-6

Dedicated to my mom and dad,
Rita and Robert McColl.
Rita McColl represents the states
of being of unconditional love,
generosity, caring, kindness, friendliness
and warmth, and Robert McColl
represents the states of being of
playfulness, fun, humor, intelligence,
unconditional love and giving.

Acknowledgments

In my life I have been blessed with many people who have been great support and inspiration to me, and I would like to express my thanks to them.

My son Michel, my greatest inspiration and my greatest joy, in his own gentle and loving way reminds me of the gifts that I am blessed to teach others. He shows me the mirror image of my own states of being and inspires me to always stay true to who I am.

My sister Judy McColl for being an incredible support and continually showing me that I can count on her. For being an example of the highest level of the states of determination, giving, honesty and caring.

My brother Bob McColl and sister-in-law Alice McColl for being wonderful role models and for demonstrating perfect examples of devotion and patience.

My brother Gary McColl, who is no longer with us here on earth, but remains in our hearts forever, for being the best source of laughter and humor in my life.

Anick Lavoie, a true and special friend, has answers any time and every time I need them. I am grateful to her for being there for me; I know that I can count on her for her undying friendship and support. She is never judgmental, always loving, gently putting me back on track when I stray from my path.

Neale Donald Walsch, who has uniquely touched my life, teaching me and reminding me of the wisdom of the Universe.

Deepak Chopra, one of my greatest Master Teachers, through his phenomenal teachings, opening my eyes to unlimited possibilities and providing the source to get in touch with my soul.

And to Diane Craig, supporting me all the way, never wavering. Being a true friend and a wonderful loving and giving person.

Thank you to Wayne Dyer for his phenomenal books, audio programs and seminars, reminding me of things that I hadn't realized that I had forgotten.

My extreme gratitude to Kathy Buckley for being the source of inspiration, humor and laughter that she unconditionally provides me with.

A special thanks to my extraordinary and loving friends Judith Yaworsky, Marie Allard, Craig Senior, Jane Pick, Suzanne and Bryon Petti, Colleen Moore, Barry Doucette, Brenda and Tom Moss, and Val McInnis, who encouraged me, helped me and are a constant and never-ending support.

To Bob Proctor a special "thank you" for opening up the flow of energy that had been blocked for so many years and for showing me the way to my unlimited potential.

To Tony Robbins, who helped me find my path when I got lost. For giving so much of himself to make an enormous and positive difference in my life and for enriching the lives of millions of people around the world. Tony is an outstanding role model for passion, absolute commitment, perseverance and certainty.

An enormous and heartfelt gratitude to a special friend Paul Montelongo, who has helped me maintain my focus, reminded me of the purpose of my life, encouraged me through adversity and supported me in more ways than he knows.

To Janet Shorten, the editor of this book, who helped me achieve my goal of "having my book edited by one of the best editors in the world!"

To Fernando Martinez, whose heart and soul goes into his work because he has a genuine desire to help others. Thank you for your commitment and your hard work to help create the perfect images and valuable services for the website.

To the many other masters and experts to whom I am truly and deeply grateful, who have taught me their wisdom and applied knowledge: Jack Canfield, Mark Victor Hansen, Marianne Williamson and Louise Hay.

Foreword

By Bob Proctor
Author of the best-selling book *You Were Born Rich*

O ver the past 33 years, I have conducted seminars worldwide helping people to understand the wondrous potential of their marvelous mind. In 1980, I was contracted by a Canadian corporation to speak at a convention and then conduct a series of seminars for their company across the country. It was a dynamic, young, fast-moving organization that was marketing word processors, a relatively new concept in the marketplace at that time. They attracted many dynamic individuals, one of whom was Peggy McColl.

In the seminars, as I began explaining the workings of the mind, how paradigms are formed and how they can be changed, this young lady's eyes began to glow. It was obvious the information was falling into place for her and her performance began to skyrocket.

Off and on, over the past 20 years, I have kept in touch with Peggy and was always very pleased to find that she had never stopped studying and even more importantly, never ceased applying what she had learned. The information that she is sharing has been tried and tested; it works! It is indeed a pleasure for me to write the foreword to this book.

Over the past 40 years, I have picked up and read countless thousands of books on human potential and personal growth. After a while, you begin to develop a sense for the books that make a difference and the ones that don't. I can assure you, this book has the potential to impact your life in a very positive way. You will feel the changes take place inside of you as you begin to digest and get emotionally involved with many of the beautiful truths that you will find in each chapter.

The great German philosopher Goethe clearly explained where we must begin if we truly desire to improve the quality of our life. He said, "Before you can do something, you first must be something." Goethe was right and Peggy McColl has learned that lesson well. Step by step, idea by idea, Peggy began to alter her old conditioning and the inner changes she made were reflected in the results she achieved. Her book *On Being...The Creator of Your Destiny* is a step-by-step program that you can follow that will take you to whatever goal you establish. She has obviously journalled the changes she has made in her own life and is sharing with the reader how to establish and alter primary causes, thereby creating permanent changes in results.

This book should actually be studied, chapter by chapter. And, while you are studying it, attempt to remember something this author learned some 20 years ago: that no amount of reading or memorizing will improve the quality of a person's life. It is the understanding and application of wise thoughts that count. Understanding can only come through study. The information between the covers of this book contains power, possibility and promise.

Change is inevitable; you see it everywhere, every day. However, personal growth is a choice...it's a choice each of us must make, personally and privately. I encourage you to make that choice now.

In Chapter 2, Peggy quotes one of my favorite authors, James Allen. In his marvelous little book, *As a Man Thinketh*, Allen explains, "People are anxious to improve their circumstances, but unwilling to improve themselves. They therefore remain bound." You are a spiritual being; the essence of you is perfect. The purpose of all life is to bring that perfection to the surface of our conscious awareness. The results we are achieving in the various areas of our life are a reflection of the inner progress we are making.

Permit me to suggest that as you turn to the first chapter in this book, you make an irrevocable decision to become all you are capable of being...each day, one day at a time. Keep in mind what this author is clearly communicating: that you do create your own destiny.

Introduction

ongratulations on finding your way to this book.

You have this book in your possession for a reason. What is that reason? This may be a question that you are fully aware of and you may be looking for a definitive answer. You may in fact be looking for answers to many other questions too.

You have come to the right place. There are very clear answers in this book. All the great sayings are on your side: *"Ask and the answer shall be given you." "Seek and you shall find." "When the student is ready, the teacher will appear."*

It is possible that you are not aware of any specific reason for picking up this book. Nevertheless, you have attracted this book and this knowledge to you. And answers will be given to you, even if you haven't consciously asked the questions. You may want to consider the questions you *would* ask if you could know the answer to any question.

My best advice to you is to read this book with an open mind and an open heart. Opening up your heart and your mind will allow you to see things that you normally wouldn't see. It will allow you to consider additional possibilities that you might not have considered if your mind was in only a semi-receptive state. While you are reading, please suspend any disbelief or pre-judgments and let the ideas enter your mind.

What I am about to share with you is the result of over a quarter-century of passionate study on the subject of personal growth—also known as self-help, inspiration, motivation, reaching goals, personal development, achieving success and creating your own destiny. This book is a summary of the ideas from the "best of the best." It is a consolidation of the ideas and advice of the best personal development speakers, self-help gurus and motivational experts, who in turn have invested their lives in the study and sharing of information. This book is a summation of the findings of the many masters that I have studied. There are real gems and gold nuggets inside this book. Like gems, they only have value when they are mined, polished and possessed.

As a word of explanation to my esteemed reader, this book was written in a spiritual tone and has intentionally left out any reference to any particular deity in an effort to respect your own spiritual beliefs. Based on your own beliefs, insert or substitute the spiritual identity that you are most comfortable with whenever you come across references to God, the Creator or the Universe.

For every disciplined effort there is a multiple reward.
Jim Rohn

—✦—

My story

Why did I dedicate over a quarter of a century to the study of personal development, personal growth and self-help? Because I had a deep desire to get out of my own self-created personal pain.

In 1980 I made a very firm decision: a decision to get some answers for myself on why my life wasn't working; a decision to eliminate the pain in my life and to be happy; a decision to stop blaming others for the lack of fulfillment in my life; a decision to take responsibility.

I have bought and read hundreds of books on the subject of personal development. I have purchased thousands of audio cassette programs and numerous video products. I've traveled the world to attend seminars and hear some of the greatest speakers and authors. I was desperately seeking answers. And did I find them? Yes, everywhere I went. Now I'm going to share them with you in simple terms, and provide you with practical tools for your own personal development.

What inspired me to write this book?

The creation of this book comes from a very simple and basic desire—a desire to help others who may be in similar painful states, or destructive states of being. I have developed such a strong passion for personal, professional and corporate development that I have built my business around it—helping individuals and corporations succeed.

As you consider the ideas you are about to encounter, and as you move through your own evolution, I invite you to use the strategies from this book as a guide to support you. Consider this book to be your personal development guide to creating your destiny.

My philosophy in life is to keep things simple. You will find that the book follows that philosophy. One of the things that I know for certain is that life doesn't have to be complicated. The process of creating your reality is common sense; the process of creating your destiny is simple. You decide whether you are going to take the long road, *complexity*, or the shorter route, *simplicity*.

Creating an ultimate destiny and living the life of your dreams is not a skill reserved for a select few. Everyone has the same energy system available to them. This book will teach you how to access your energy and become the creator of your ideal reality.

SECTION 1

On Being...

Aware

- 1 -

Is This Magic?

$\mathcal{A}$ wise man once said: "Magic is the opposite of Life! With magic, when you know how it works, the magic goes away. With life, when you know how it works, the magic begins."

Is it really magic when you start to get your life working for you? When you achieve your goals and start to live the life of your dreams? Is it magic when you stop the dissatisfaction in your life, or the pain in your heart, and begin to feel joyful and happy? Is it magic to be able to create any result that you choose? Or become a master at handling adversity so that it is positive and empowering for you and for others?

No, but its appearance is magic! When you understand how to get life working for you, you can make that magic appear for you. You can,

---

through applying the knowledge in this book, learn how to live the life that you desire. You can learn to live in happiness, joy and love, with peace and serenity.

Buying personal development books and reading them will not necessarily bring you the things you desire. It is the understanding and the application that will make the difference and turn your dreams into reality.

When you are reading this book and you discover a great idea, take action. Stay committed to your path. Understanding and applying this process, reshaping your life through your creative ability, is supremely fulfilling. Once you have put the process in motion, it sets up its own momentum. You will learn more about creating momentum as you go through the book.

Whatever the mind of man can conceive
and believe it can achieve.
Napoleon Hill

—✦—

How do you get started?

Decide. If you picked up this book and started to read it, you may have already made a decision to take action. You will start to move in a new direction when you decide to do so. People cannot be forced to make changes in their life if they do not want to. "You can lead a horse to water, but you can't make him drink." There must be a desire and there must be discipline. But desire and discipline do not mean difficulty. Change can be made with *ease*. Force will not work either. Do not try to force things to be created. This process works best when you apply action with faith.

Make your own personal commitment to follow through, and not only read and absorb this material but apply it as you go through the process described in the chapters ahead.

– 2 –

Awareness

*T*he next step, after decision, is awareness. Awareness is noticing the realities of the experiences that you have created for yourself. Awareness requires that you do not judge your results, or anyone else's results, for that matter. Awareness is not about feeling guilt, shame, embarrassment or resentment. The past is the past and you cannot change it, but you can learn from it. And you can change the way you look at the past. Therefore, do not seek to forget the past; learn from it and seek to change the future.

Many people are traveling along the road of life and stop themselves when they find a fictitious hurdle or an imaginary barricade in front of them. What is this imaginary road block? The road block is their own creation, formed by looking at past results and making a decision not to move forward. Perhaps it is a belief that they are not good enough to be wealthy, or famous, or loved—a belief that comes from the past. But where is the past? Behind us. And that is where it is meant to stay.

If you feel dissatisfied with past results, or if you believe you have hurt others or you have hurt yourself, acknowledge that, learn from it and make a new decision not to repeat it. Awareness can have tremendous power when you use it to serve you.

Also, do not blame another for your pain or for the results in your life. In some way, consciously or subconsciously, you have attracted every event to you and your life. Nobody *does* anything *to* you. No one *makes* you do anything that you don't, at some level, choose to do. No one makes you feel anything. You decide, and you alone, what you are going to feel, whether you are conscious of this or not. No one has power over you unless you give it to him or her. If you find yourself uttering the words "you made me feel," or "look what he/she did to me," recognize that you are in denial. (And denial is not a river in Egypt.)

Move out of pain

If you would like to move out of pain, then stop living your life by focusing on your past or blaming others. Learn from your past, make new choices and move on. A person living in the past is like a driver who is driving down the road staring in the rear-view mirror. Sooner or later, driving in this manner will lead to catastrophe. Allow the past to serve its rightful purpose as awareness and understanding. Your past does not determine your future.

Become aware

How do you become aware? By focusing on what you are thinking, doing and creating.

Think of it this way: you may be aware most of the time, but you are not aware that you are aware. Let's use a simple example. Right now you are breathing and you know that you are breathing. Now become aware of your breathing. Listen to your breath as you inhale and exhale. Notice the rhythm and the depth of your breathing. Now you are aware of your breathing. Before I suggested that you become aware of your breathing, you were subconsciously aware that you were breathing, but may not have been consciously aware of it.

People don't need only to think. People need to be aware of what they are thinking. These are two distinct functions.

As you are going through this book, be aware of the thoughts and feelings you are experiencing. Be aware of the decisions you are making, or may have made in the past. Be aware of the new choices you are making and the opportunities these new choices represent. Be aware of the challenges or obstacles that you are facing now, may have faced in the past, and may possibly face in the future.

A large number of people are aware of what they are creating but do nothing about it. Others, the enlightened ones, are aware of what they are creating, aware that they may be creating undesirable outcomes, and they make new decisions to create new results without guilt or resentment. Guilt is a destructive emotion. Harboring guilt or resentment toward another is equivalent to your taking poison and expecting it to hurt another.

My belief is that everything in life is perfection, and there are no coincidences. There are definite circumstances in which we may not understand or see the perfection, but if we believe it to be there, we'll find it. If you are not happy with the results that you have had in your life up until now, be grateful for those results and experiences. They are true gifts. They are revealing important messages to you.

Recognize that you will have adversity and challenges. The most important thing to remember is that it is okay to "go down"; just don't stay down. Practice being strong during the great times, so that when you do experience challenges in your life you'll be able to manage them with more ease.

Do not ignore your challenges, expecting them to disappear. Putting a lid on your challenges is equivalent to throwing garbage into a garbage can and expecting it to disappear because the lid is on the can. Sooner or later the lid will come off and the result will not be pleasant.

Recognize the gift of past experiences; give thanks for them, and move forward with your head held high. Today is a new day. This day is a day full of opportunities to create yourself and your results anew. Take charge of your life today and every day, moving forward. Stay strong and be persistent and diligent in your approach. You will, I promise you, start to see significant positive results in your life within a short time.

Why do people continue to get what they've always got?

The answer to this question is simple: "If you continue to do what you've always done, you'll continue to get what you've always got." Or, to expand this statement: "If you continue to be who you have always been, you'll continue to have what you've always had." If we don't like what we are getting, we need to look at what it is that we are doing. Or better yet, we need to look at who and what we are *being*.

Your past does not define who you are. It may define who you were being at that time, or prior to that time, but *who you are* is a day-by-day creation. That creation is the process this book will guide you through.

If you wake up every day and you think the same thoughts, do the same things, say the same words, out loud or internally, you will create the same results. It is not "same old, same old." It is a new creation, but it may not appear to be a new creation because you are doing, being, thinking the "same old, same old."

People are looking for something outside of themselves to make them feel a certain feeling. As long as you look for something outside of yourself to bring you something, you'll never get this process working for you.

> *People are anxious to improve their circumstances, but unwilling*
> *to improve themselves. They therefore remain bound.*
> James Allen

People frequently want to improve their circumstances but do nothing about it. Consequently, things get worse.

Why does doing nothing make things worse? Because things do not stay the same. Everything is changing in the universe. Everything is energy in motion, either moving forward or moving backward, either getting better or getting worse. In which direction would you like to go?

If you would like things, experiences, events in your life to change, if you would like your results to change, first *you* must change.

People make a decision to take charge of their life when they are dissatisfied with their life. People make a decision to change when they are in pain.

The length of time that it takes to come to that decision depends on the level of dissatisfaction or the depth of the pain or the level of commitment. When you hear someone say, "That's it, I've had enough!" you may be fairly sure they are ready for change. Other indicators are "I'm sick and tired," "I'm no longer going to live my life like this," "I've got to do something about my life." When you hear people, or yourself, say these words with conviction, you'll know they, or you, are ready for change.

But dissatisfaction isn't the only instigator of change. Perhaps you simply want to recognize your power as a creator in your own life.

SECTION 2

On Being...

A Creator

- 3 -

The Energy Source

*Y*ou are a creative being and you play a role in creating your reality every minute of every day. Most people are unaware of this simple truth. Ignoring this truth can cause you to miss out on experiences that you would like to have in your life. Becoming aware of this truth, and how this process works, will allow you to create extraordinary results.

You have available to you four levels of creative energy. These four levels of creative energy are **thought, word, action** and **being**. This section will explain how these creative energies operate and how you can get them to work for you.

One of these four is more powerful than the others: **being** has great creative energy. The energy level of being transcends the other three levels (a more detailed explanation is found in Chapter 11).

Every one of us has these four levels of energy. The difference is in how people use it. This energy source is unlimited and always available.

Like the electricity that is delivered to your home, the universal energy is always available and there is an infinite supply. Whether you use it or not is up to you. If you do want to utilize the universal energy, you simply tap into it or turn it up.

Imagine a dimmer switch. The more brightness you desire, the higher you move the switch. The limit to the brightness is the position that you choose to set the dimmer control. If you place the dimmer control at the highest setting, you will experience the greatest brightness.

Keep in mind that the energy is available and will respond regardless of where you place the dimmer control. Therefore, you can decide how much of that energy you will use and when you will use it.

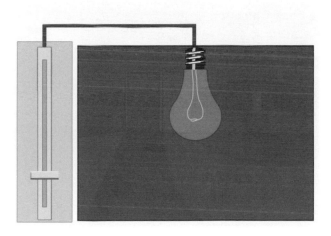

In this example the dimmer control switch is on low; therefore, very little energy is being utilized and the result is very little brightness.

In this example, the dimmer control is closer to the highest setting; therefore, the light bulb provides increased brightness.

In this example, the dimmer control is at the maximum capacity; therefore, the light bulb is fully illuminated and provides a result that has additional opportunities.

These three illustrations represent the result of tapping into the universal energy at different levels, as demonstrated by setting the dimmer switch. You control your own dimmer switch, or energy level, with your thoughts, words, actions and your states of being.

If you choose not to use the energy of the universe, or if you are not aware of the energy available, you may be living your life according to someone else's plan. That is not necessarily a bad thing. But it is for you, and you only, to decide whose plan you will follow.

Get in touch with your energy. This is the secret to everything, to all your creativity and your magnificence. You are creative and the Universe is creative.

Everything that has been created, all material things, come from the same universal source. Nature responds to creative energy and will produce results by manifesting thoughts into form. We will know this to be true through our own experience and we will know it to be true by witnessing other people's experiences. As a result, we can fulfill any desire and experience fulfillment to any extent that we desire.

To dream anything that you want to dream; that is the
beauty of the human mind. To do anything that you want to do;
that is the strength of the human will. To trust yourself to
test your limits; that is the courage to succeed.
Bernard Edmonds

—❦—

– 4 –

The Power of Thought

Every thought you think is energy in motion. The thought, as energy, goes out into the universe and goes on forever.

I'm certain you have heard the expression "Be careful what you think about." Once you think a thought, it leaves your mind and begins to work with the natural laws of the universe. The primary laws that work with thought are the Law of Attraction and the Law of Gestation.

The Law of Attraction takes that thought, and starts to draw energy to you to manifest that thought into form.

The Law of Gestation dictates that there is a period of time that must elapse before that thought will manifest in form. The length of that time is dependent on the magnitude and intensity of the energy of the thought.

These universal laws take something that is non-material, specifically thought, and move it into material form.

The universe does not distinguish between a thought that is positive and one that is negative. A thought is like a seed that is planted in the ground. The universe will provide the seed with the energy to manifest that thought into material form. Mother Nature, who is also natural energy, does not care if it is the seed of a weed or the seed of a flower. It will begin to grow. How well it will grow will depend on a number of other elements—for example, how much additional energy the seed/thought is given.

Let's use the example of a good thought, something that would serve you and be supportive. Consider thinking, "I can do anything I set my mind to." This may be a thought that you have decided to think for the first time. In other words, it may not be typical for you to think this way, or common to your previous thought patterns; nevertheless, it is now energy in motion.

If you didn't have that thought again and you continued to think in a negative fashion, you would continue to draw energy similar to the negative thoughts in your mind. However, if you thought "I can do anything I set my mind to," and you repeated that, and made it a consistent thought, you would start to experience new feelings, take new actions, think additional positive thoughts, and begin to produce positive results because you are now moving energy in a new direction. You have planted a new seed-thought and you have continued to send it energy to help it grow.

Why? Because you are using the energy of the universe, namely *thought*. Since you are repeating the thought with conviction (increased intensity) and you are repeating the thought over and over again, you are re-energizing yourself for a new result. The level of intensity is in direct proportion to the feeling of passion. The more passionate you are, the more intensity you will have. The less passion you have, the less the intensity.

You can have anything you want—if you want it badly enough.
You can be anything you want to be, do anything you set out to accom-
plish, if you hold to that desire with singleness of purpose.
Abraham Lincoln

—✦—

Conscious thought

You, and you alone, decide what to think. This is the truth. There is no one in your brain deciding what you are going to think. If you want to take control of your own thinking, become aware of what you are thinking. Start to think about what you are thinking about. And when you notice a negative or destructive thought enter your mind, think again. Think a new thought, an empowering thought, a thought that supports what you would like to experience or create in your life. Keep thinking those supportive, positive and empowering thoughts repeatedly.

Thought creates a flow of energy. Your thoughts, as well as everyone else's thoughts, are energy in motion. You may not visibly see this energy flow, but it is happening nevertheless. Thought energy is omnipresent. It is outside of you, inside of you, in the room, outside of the room, inside another, outside another, in the universe. Thought energy is everywhere. We tap into this thought energy with our con-sciousness. You need to be aware of this energy because it is creative energy and it has an effect on your life. Therefore, when you tap into positive energy you experience positive results; similarly, when you tap into negative energy you experience negative results. This is the primary reason for becoming aware of your consistent thoughts, whether they are positive or negative. Thinking negative thoughts pro-duces negative results. Thinking positive thoughts produces positive results.

In addition to noticing your consistent thoughts, also notice the words you are speaking, notice the actions you are taking, notice your behav-ior and your feelings. If you know that your words, actions, behavior and your feelings are not supportive, use the energy of thought to start a new process of creation.

Recommendation: The next time you become aware that you are feel-ing a negative emotion, notice what your thoughts are at that moment. Change your thoughts to positive thoughts and you will start to feel dif-ferent. Repeat this process over and over again, thinking only those thoughts that you want to or choose to experience—namely, positive and supportive thoughts.

Subconscious thought

Subconscious thoughts reside deep within, in what is known as your subconscious mind. An idea becomes subconscious as a result of thoughts that are accepted over and over again.

What goes into your subconscious mind comes through your conscious mind. As adults we decide what ideas and thoughts we will allow into our mind. As young children we have not fully developed our reasoning faculties and so allow most things to go into our subconscious mind. A child is wide open and receptive to thoughts. Therefore, a child's belief system is created at a very young age.

Your subconscious mind is a repository of memories of all of the events that you have experienced in your life up until now, as well as thoughts and ideas. Your subconscious mind is always collecting; it accepts whatever you give it, whether that is a healthy thought or a destructive thought. The subconscious mind will access the old memories upon your request or as a reflex reaction. When memories are accessed they re-enter your subconscious mind and help to reinforce your beliefs. These beliefs may have taken a short period of time to create (seconds), or they may be deeply embedded beliefs that you have created and recreated again and again.

The subconscious mind is very powerful. When we understand how it works, we can start to make conscious decisions about what we will create in our subconscious mind and what we will access from our subconscious mind.

You may have experienced this situation: all of a sudden you feel a terrible thought arise in your conscious mind. You say to yourself, "Where did that come from?" It invariably came from your subconscious mind.

All of your beliefs are embedded in your subconscious mind. Let me give you an example. Let us say you have a belief that "most people cannot be trusted," and you don't know where that belief came from. It has probably been created in your subconscious mind. But how did that belief come to be in your subconscious mind? It may have come from a childhood experience, a number of movies, books about infidelity, stories about dishonest people, magazine covers that you saw in the grocery store, overheard conversations of others speaking about people who couldn't be trusted and claiming to have valid proof. You may not know where that idea came from, but at some point it was accepted into your subconscious mind and has been reinforced by further acceptance of related ideas to become a belief.

Because your subconscious mind is so powerful, you will view the world based on your beliefs. You will see the world through the filters of your belief systems and make decisions accordingly.

Some people completely lose sight of reality because of the beliefs they have created. Some people have created beliefs that are absolutely absurd. These people are living in their own little world. Or they go through life in a fog, unable to see clearly.

If, as a child, you had a Mr. Potato Head, you will recall that you could make up different faces for Mr. Potato Head by putting on different eyes, nose, mouth, glasses, mustache, ears, hair, hats, et cetera. When I speak to audiences I sometimes bring my Mr. Potato Head with me. I'll talk about people who have set up beliefs in their subconscious minds that don't allow them to see the obvious, and it is at that point that I'll remove Mr. Potato Head's eyes and say, "this is the way those types of people go through life."

Your beliefs can set up blinders, or blockages, and you will then miss out on so many of life's wonderful opportunities. For example, a workaholic may believe that her career is more important than her family and may be blind to the effects her work addiction is having on her family, until one day she wakes up and she is alone. However, a critical moment can cause a person to remove their blinders, or clear their fog, and start to see the new opportunities and the world of unlimited possibilities. It all starts with choice.

The good news is that you can change your subconscious mind by choosing new thoughts over and over again. You then ultimately replace old beliefs with new beliefs.

Philosophy of a Winner

If you think you are beaten, you are.
If you think you dare not, you don't.
If you like to win, but you think you can't
It is almost certain you won't.
If you think you'll lose you've lost.
For out in the world we find,
Success begins with a person's will;
It's all in the state of mind.
If you think you're outclassed, you are.
You've got to think high to rise.
You've got to be sure of yourself
Before you can win a prize.
Life's battles don't always go
To the strongest woman or man,
But sooner or later, if you're going to win,
You have to think you can.

—Adaptation of a poem by Waler D. Wintle

– 5 –

Self Talk

*S*elf talk occurs in your conscious mind and has an impact on your subconscious mind when repeated over and over again. Repeating self talk is one very effective method of creating beliefs.

Everyone talks to himself or herself. Most people have an internal dialogue occurring most of their waking hours, whether they are consciously aware of it or not. This is called self talk. Your self talk consists of the thoughts you are having within your mind to yourself, about yourself. Self talk is your internal communication and it, too, is creative energy in motion.

Self talk uses the energy of thought. Self talk can either build or destroy your self-esteem. Your self-esteem is your own evaluation or judgment of yourself. Your self-esteem will have an effect on your life and your results.

Let's review the different types of self talk.

Negative self talk that you accept

The most detrimental and harmful form of self talk takes place when you say something negative about yourself, either vocally or via internal dialogue, *and* you accept it.

Let me share a personal experience of this type of self talk. Recently a friend of mine was sitting beside me while I was searching for a file on my laptop computer. As I was searching for this file, I made an error and said out loud, "You dummy." I was playfully referring to myself. My friend immediately piped up and said, "Don't talk to my friend like that!" I appreciated the support of my friend and at the same time I realized how we often say things like that to ourselves, without realizing the impact.

This type of self talk is destructive and we need to be aware of it. When you use this type of self talk, first become aware of what you are saying. Then choose replacement self talk that is positive and supportive.

Indicators of this type of negative self talk are phrases such as:
"I can't..."
"I don't have the energy/knowledge/ability to do that."
"I could *never* do that."
"I don't have what it takes."
"I'm useless."
"No matter what I try, I can never lose weight."

This kind of talk is poison to our self-esteem, whether we say it silently to ourselves, or out loud to someone else about ourselves.

This kind of self talk needs to be stopped immediately and eliminated from your vocabulary. If you hear yourself using this type of self talk, immediately put a stop to it. If you put poison in your water would you drink it? No, so don't poison your mind.

Replace the negative self talk above with the following positive self talk:
"I can and I will..."
"I do have an abundance of energy/knowledge/ability to do that."
"I can do that."
"I do have what it takes."

"I'm valuable, worthwhile, a contributor."
"I see myself losing weight now."

Negative talk by others to you

Have you ever seen a child plugging their ears because they don't want to hear what someone is saying to them?

Parents need to realize the impact their words can have on their children and choose more carefully. One day I was waiting for a friend on a street in an upper-middle-class suburb. I was parked with the car turned off, simply watching the activities on the street. Within a few minutes, a mother, father and little boy walked down the sidewalk. I could see that the father was yelling at his young son, and even though I couldn't hear what he was saying, I could see the effects on the young boy. The little boy was visibly shriveling and cowering as he walked a few paces behind, and I felt his pain.

My belief is there are other ways of delivering the message to our children, and it can be done effectively with love and respect. Similarly, we can talk to other adults in a positive and supportive way.

When people believe they are being loving, and they are saying negative and hurtful things to you, you may not want to hear it, because it is natural to obstruct pain from our lives. However, the words we hear others say to us do not have to be painful. We are at choice whether another person's words are painful to us or not. If someone says something to you that is cruel, do not allow those words to enter your mind; immediately reject them. Most people forget about the choices that we have, and choice is one of our greatest gifts.

I have seen the self-esteem of countless numbers of people dramatically affected by the acceptance of what others say to them as truth, when the words are negative and destructive. On the other hand, accepting others' comments or words as true when they are positive can be a liberating experience and not a debilitating experience. But regardless of what others say, negative or positive, we have the ability to choose whether we are going to accept it or not. Reject any negative talk from others. Accept the positive.

People tend to accept the words of others when they see the person speaking the words as an authority figure, such as mother, father, older sibling, teacher or clergyman. Negative words from these people are the most challenging kind of negativity to reject because people do believe and have respect for the other person. But that does not mean that the person's negative words are accurate. You must still reject this type of self talk. Or listen to what may be true. For example, it is possible that the person saying negative things to you is fearful, or they may be concerned for you. What they have said may be something they believe to be true. If the latter is the case, and there is a lesson in their words, consider the observation, learn from it, and make new choices.

– 6 –

The Power of Word

*T*houghts expressed verbally—using words—form the second level of creation. The words you say out loud to yourself or to others build on the flow of thought energy that is already in motion.

The actual and specific words that you say also affect the intensity of the energy. For example, if you have a strong desire to have something in your life, using the words "I wish I had that" or "I believe I will have that" or "I know I'll have it" will each have a different impact on the outcome. The words "I wish" are not as strong as the words "I believe," but the words with the ultimate intensity are "I know."

Notice the words that you are saying to others. Are you a positive person, or a negative person? It is easy to determine the answer by simply listening to the words you are using.

When you are asked the question "How are you?" how do you respond? There is a difference between how you will feel when you respond with "I'm okay" and how you will feel when you respond, "I'm feeling wonderful!"

Some words are empowering and some words are destructive. The following is a list of energizing and empowering words:

Know	Infinite	Certain
Believe	Empowered	Enlightened

| Love | Wonderful | Magnificent |
| Create | Meaningful | Truth |

Use positive and emotionally charged words. Create the vocabulary of a confident and faithful person.

Word energy elements
The energy of words is affected by the following elements: tonality, intensity, language, volume and repetition.

Tonality
Tonality refers to the way you say something. Where you put the emphasis or how you say the words can have an impact on the meaning or interpretation of the words. Listen to where you are putting emphasis and if it appears to be destructive or negative in any way, change it. And listen to your tone of voice, and if it appears to be negative or unpleasant, change it.

Intensity
Intensity will increase or decrease the power of the words' energy. Use intensity to your advantage when you speak with positive and empower-ing words. For example, when you are using "I am" statements to rein-force or build a belief, say the words with intensity and it will increase the effect on your belief.

Language
We will use "language" to refer to the words that you use when you speak. It is possible that you will feel certain things when you use cer-tain words. For example, if you were upset and you said the words "I am really pissed off!" those words would cause you to feel angry, and depending on the intensity and tonality, you might feel extremely angry. But if, instead of saying the words "I'm really pissed off!" you said "I am a little annoyed," and you said it with no intensity, or very little

intensity, you would likely feel only a little annoyed. Or you could say "I don't understand," because sometimes when we are angry it's because we don't have all of the information and we have created a belief before we have gathered all the facts.

A number of years ago a friend of mine constantly said the words, "I never meet men." I finally told her that she was getting exactly what she was claiming, specifically, never meeting men. I suggested she change her thoughts, words and actions and start to focus on meeting men. She did change her language and has now developed the art of meeting men; she happily claims that she is meeting men everywhere she goes.

Volume
Like intensity, language and tonality, volume will create different emotions based on the loudness or softness of the words you speak. For example, if you were to say the words "I am so happy!" and you said the words loudly, you would feel different than if you said "I am so happy" quietly.

Repetition
This one element alone will have a dramatic effect on your life and your results. When we speak words over and over again, we reinforce our belief system. In turn, we take actions, think thoughts and create the results. Watch your dialogue. Pay attention to the words that are coming out of your mouth. Notice what you are saying over and over again. Monitor the words, and the tonality, intensity, volume and repetition of the words.

Understand the power of words and use this energy to create results. Speak words that are loving, if you choose to experience love in your life. Speak the words of a successful person, if you choose to experience success in your life. Say the words of confidence, if you choose to be a confident person.

– 7 –

Affirmations

*T*he strongest statement that you can make is an "I am" statement. Learn to think positively about yourself through positive affirmations. Making "I am" statements opens up the channel to your consciousness (both conscious and subconscious) to build new beliefs. When you hear yourself say "I am...," listen to the words that follow. Quite often we hear people say "I am sick and tired." Or "I am so fed up." Or "I am going out of my mind." Watch for those negative affirmations about yourself, other people and the world. Whether you are making negative comments about yourself, which are the most detrimental, or negative comments about others and other things, you are causing *dis*-ease in your body.

Affirmations are positive statements that you can place on your bathroom mirror to read in the morning while you are getting ready for the day and in the evening just before going to bed. They will set your attitude for the day. You can also take them with you wherever you go. Attitude is a little thing that makes a big difference to your life.

Here are some examples of positive affirmations:

I have unlimited potential. I have the ability to create anything that I desire in my life. I am one with the Universe.

I am an Olympic athlete. I am the best in the world in my sport.

I have excellent powers of focus. Each day I consciously work to improve and perfect my ability to direct and hold my concentration.

When I decide to focus on a thing, I give it my complete attention.

I am able to easily visualize my desired result in advance.

Every day I visualize the achievement of my goals. I create complete detailed scenes in my mind of myself succeeding. I see the scenes over and over again, each time more clearly, and I begin to create that future event in my mind.

Each day I get even better at clearly visualizing the best of myself and my future in my own mind. I visualize it, I act on it and I make it happen.

I think, act, walk, talk, breathe, move, gesture and perform like a champion in all that I do.

I set my goals and I reach them. Success is a way of life for me.

I am in outstanding physical, emotional and psychological condition. I only feed my body those foods that are nutritious and good for me.

I am resourceful. I have the ability to do whatever it takes to succeed.

I have tremendous confidence in my talents and my abilities.

I am committed to perform with excellence in all that I do.

I am a giver and what I give comes back to me multiplied.

A Creator

I have drive, spirit, stamina and endurance. I have an outstanding winning attitude about myself and about everything I do.

I know that I am headed in the right, winning direction. I learn from the past and look forward.

My gratitude opens me up to unlimited success.

I deeply respect my body and take excellent care of it each day.

I feel great pleasure from the health and strength of my physical body.

I start each day and continue throughout the day with an abundance of energy.

I can do it and I will do it!

I have all of the resources to reach my goals.

Everything I need is within me now!

I am totally focused and can clearly see my outcome.

I have the ability to do whatever it takes to succeed, and to support all those whom I love.

I am successful in every way.

My work is a great contribution to others, and I am richly rewarded for it.

My gratitude opens me up to unlimited financial success.

I feel prosperous and I think prosperous thoughts.

I handle and invest my money wisely, and I profit daily.

I feel great pleasure as I take massive action to accomplish my goals.

I live each day with an attitude of gratitude.

I have faith in God and I have faith in myself.

It is spiritual to be abundant and I know that the Universe wants me to enjoy all if its riches. I accept with gratitude.

I am worthy of receiving all that I desire.

I deserve to succeed in all areas of my life.

I am confident, determined and persistent.

I am a "do-it-now!" person, and I make my time serve me.

I am abundantly wealthy.

I am successful beyond my wildest dreams in all areas of my life and a true example of possibility.

I am unconditionally loving.

I am eternally grateful for all of the gifts in my life.

I am successful in my business and I am enjoying my success.

I invest quality time with my family and friends.

I have an excellent understanding of effective investment strategies and I utilize them to constantly increase my investment portfolio and reap the financial benefits.

I am fit and energetic.

I am a great support for my family.

I am extremely creative.

I am completely loved.

I am completely lovable.

– 8 –

Beliefs

A belief starts with the acceptance of information repeatedly taken in through your conscious mind and then embedded in your subconscious mind.

Beliefs play a vital role in all of our actions, our behaviors and, ultimately, our results. Whatever we believe becomes our reality. We filter all events through our beliefs. We make decisions based on our beliefs. We treat others based on our beliefs. All of our actions, all of our behaviors, all of our results are consistent with our beliefs.

We create our own beliefs. We can create beliefs that support us, or beliefs that do not support us.

Beliefs determine:
- the meaning we link to an event
- the questions we ask ourselves
- the choices we make
- the actions we take
- what we choose to focus on
- what we choose to not focus on
- how we react to a situation
- how we feel about something
- how we receive information

- how we analyze information
- how we treat others.

Supportive beliefs

Beliefs that are supportive will help to take us in the direction of our goals. All of the goals that we set and achieve will be based on the supportive beliefs that we have. For example, if we have a belief that "I am intelligent," then we will act and behave in the manner of an intelligent person. More importantly, we will realize the rewards of an intelligent person.

Recently a friend of mine was visiting from out of town. She was an exercise fanatic. When I asked why she exercised as much as she did she responded with "I have no choice." She built this belief because of the history of heart disease in her family. She believed that if she didn't exercise she would have heart problems. This is an example of a belief that served her.

Non-supportive beliefs

Beliefs that do not support us by taking us in the direction of our goals are non-supportive or destructive beliefs. Some of these beliefs are deep-rooted; they need to be uprooted and replaced with new, supportive and empowering beliefs. The non-supportive or negative beliefs are also known as *baggage*. Baggage carried forward causes delay and degradation, and can sometimes completely sabotage the end result.

An example of a non-supportive belief is "people can't be trusted" or "this can't work because it has never been done before" or "the environment/industry/economy is devastated/destroyed." A negative belief can have a substantial effect on the result, depending on the strength of the belief.

Non-supportive and limiting beliefs hold us back so that we cannot move forward in our life. Negative, non-supportive beliefs are destructive and can sabotage our ability to achieve our goals. Being clear on what these destructive beliefs are gives us tremendous power. This allows us to face the beliefs that have been keeping us from our joy and happiness. A two-part saying applies well to beliefs: "What you resist, persists" and "What you look at, disappears."

Having limiting beliefs can also block our minds from allowing any new ideas or new possibilities to be considered. It is not a matter of not being able to accept more—we simply reject. Think of the metaphor of your mind as a bottomless container; you can always put more in and the container will never fill up. The limiting belief is like Cellophane on top of your mind; when you try to pour more in, it simply won't go in.

Let's now take an honest look at those limiting beliefs in order to eliminate them from our lives.

How do we create our beliefs?

We build beliefs about many things. We build beliefs in relationship to our view of the world—our views on society, the economy, business, education, family, gender, the health system, health choices, finance, money, religion, race, our friends, our partner, and many other things, people, places and events.

If you want to know what your belief is about something or someone, it is easy to find out. Simply ask yourself several questions: "What do I think about _____? "How do I feel about _____?" "What is my gut telling me about _____?" Your answer to any of these questions, or your combined answer to all of them, is your belief.

So where do beliefs come from? Building a belief starts with a thought. The thought is considered, followed up with relevant information gathered to support the thought, then evaluated, analyzed, possibly augmented with related additional thoughts, affirmed, reaffirmed, and then, ultimately, it becomes a belief.

If we were to examine the belief "the world is a beautiful place," we would find that this belief was built once we validated the statement with additional relevant and supporting thoughts. The belief "the world is a beautiful place" might have started with seeing photographs of the many beautiful destinations in the world and could then have been supported through the experience of visiting some of these beautiful places. Or the belief "the world is a beautiful place" for you might refer to the beauty of all of the people in the world and the connection we share. It could have begun by listening to parents or religious leaders, and received support by reading inspiring stories of people's actions and experiencing meaningful interactions with others.

Beliefs about ourselves are built by affirming and reaffirming statements about ourselves and by experiences that support these statements. The belief becomes evident to others once we have built the support for that belief. We can use the example of a billboard to demonstrate the building of a belief. The poles are the support for the billboard. The billboard will not stand upright until the support columns are built. When the columns supporting the statements and experiences have been built, and are solid, the billboard will be displayed. All the world will now see the message on the billboard. This is your belief.

Our beliefs about who we are may be messages to the world, but people do not necessarily see a written message. Our personal beliefs are often communicated to others non-verbally. If you have a belief that you are a confident person, people will see that without your having to say the words "I am a confident person."

Think about the messages that you are sending to the world. Support columns are essential to support a belief. If you do not have empowering beliefs about yourself, then create new beliefs by building new supporting thoughts (columns). In time, the world will clearly see your new, positive, empowering belief.

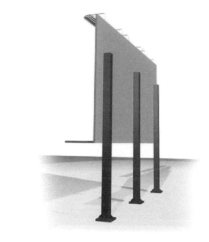

Your identity: the belief about who you are

If you were asked to define yourself, what would you say? The answer to this question will show who you believe you are. Our identity is a description of who we believe we are. Our identity is how we define ourselves.

The strongest force in human nature is the belief about who we are—our identity. Everything we do is an act of self-definition.

In order to realize a goal, you must become the type of person who would achieve that goal, by building that identity. You can build your identity with an identity statement and include "I am" statements.

The following is an example of an identity statement that was created by one of my past seminar participants. This was written in support of the goals that this individual had set.

I display and express gratitude, appreciation and thankfulness for all of the wonderful gifts in my life.

I am successful beyond my wildest dreams in all areas of my life and a true example of possibility. My life is an inspiration to others.

I love unconditionally. I am loving, determined, driven, persistent, committed, courageous, kind, confident, thoughtful, caring, warm, friendly, enthusiastic, patient, fun, resourceful, spiritual, creative, genuine, wealthy, understanding, trustworthy, generous, professional, classy, talented, brilliant, wise, healthy, sporty, toned, energetic, passionate, honest, organized, efficient, peaceful, calm and focused.

I have complete faith in God and I have complete faith in myself.

I am an outstanding, loving, nurturing, patient, kind, thoughtful, fun parent. I am a wonderful, loving, giving, committed, gentle, considerate Life Partner.

I am in great shape and I take great care of myself.

My income and my net worth are constantly increasing. I am classy and dressed impeccably at all times. I conduct myself in a professional manner at all times. I am abundantly wealthy. I have an excellent understanding of effective investment strategies

and I utilize them to constantly increase my investment
portfolio and reap the financial benefits.

I am committed to helping others by generously giving
financial contributions and time contributions.
When I make a commitment, I follow through.

I am significantly and positively making a
contribution in the lives of others.

– 9 –

The Power of Action

Faith without works is dead.
James 2:20

*T*hought and word are two powerful levels of energy. When they are combined with action, and when the energies of all three levels (thought, word, action) are moving in the same direction, you will experience incredible results.

Thinking positive, supportive, empowering thoughts and speaking affirmatively without taking action will cause you to create at a slower speed.

How does the energy of action work?

If you planted a seed in the ground and did not provide it any water, would it grow? Possibly, but it would grow much faster and become stronger and healthier if you applied the water. Giving a seed water is like taking action toward the achievement of a goal. (Additional suggestions for action toward goal achievement can be found in Section 3, On Being...Committed.)

Here is another example of how the energy of action works. When

57

you move your body, you are not moving only your physical body; you are moving energy—universal energy. Imagine a large magnet that has intense magnetic power. Imagine that the magnet is placed in a certain location and within inches of it there is a small pile of metal screws. Screws are easily attracted to the magnet. However, if we place the magnet in one location, and place the screws in another, and do nothing about moving them toward each other, we will not experience a connection, regardless of the energy that is actively working.

Result without action   Result with action

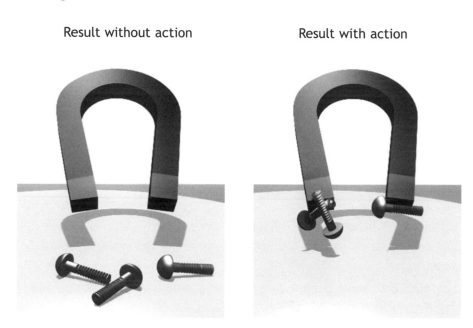

This illustrates the process of achieving our goals. The magnet represents you, the energy of the magnet represents your energy and the universal energy, and the screws represent the goal. Moving the magnet toward the goal represents your use of energy to draw your goal toward you.

If we set the goal (which starts with thought and word energy) and do not act, even though we have the energy available and we are beginning to utilize that energy, we will not get the results we desire. We must take action toward achievement of the goal.

Once a goal is set, you need to ask yourself: *What do I need to do that will take me in the direction of this goal or achieve my desired result?* You may not have the answer immediately, but keep asking the question and you will get the answer. Or seek expert advice from someone who can help you answer the question. When you keep asking the question of yourself and of another you are opening yourself up to receive the answer and to see new possibilities.

Taking action does not mean that you must take massive action. As long as you are taking some action toward your goal you will be moving in a forward direction and using the creative energy of action. Take the example of a marathon runner. Massive action could cause a new marathon trainee to burn out quickly. To learn how to be a marathon runner, you must first learn the most effective program and follow the steps in the proper sequence, then follow up with training and increase the training over a period of time. It is wiser to make steady progress consistently throughout the training and, when running a marathon, make steady progress throughout the marathon.

However, taking immediate massive action to jump-start your commitment will give you some momentum. If immediate massive action is applicable to your goal, take it, and follow up with consistent, persistent regular action. Perhaps you have seen the Successories® poster that says "SUCCESS: Some people dream about it, while others wake up and work hard at it."

You cannot expect someone else to take action for you. I'm not suggesting you don't get any assistance in taking action, but if you expect another person to do the work for you or on your behalf, the effect will be minimized.

Change the way you feel through your body movement

It has been proven that our thoughts affect the way we feel. It is also true that we can change our thoughts by changing the way we move our physical body. For example, if you have ever been depressed or stressed and you did physical exercise, you probably immediately started to feel better and think more positive thoughts.

Physical body movement and action can also assist you to move from a negative state to a positive state. The following are suggestions to help change the way you feel, by physical movement.

If you are experiencing impatience	Relax your body. Meditate. Take deep breaths from your diaphragm. Count to 10 before saying things that you may regret later.
If you are experiencing fear	Put energy in your body. Take a power walk and increase the energy as you walk. Take action toward a goal and break through the fear.
If you are experiencing stress or anxiety	Do a physical exercise that you enjoy like dancing, energy walking or swimming. Or simply try to relax your body. Find humor by reading jokes or comics. Watch a funny movie.
If you are experiencing worry	Write out positive solutions to the challenges you are facing (writing alone is a physical activity). Do something fun or something that you love to change your focus.
If you are feeling sad	Put a smile on your face. Smile at someone. Read a joke book. Share jokes. Cause someone else to smile or laugh.

– 10 –

Energy Challenges

*T*his one chapter alone is worth the price you paid for this book. One of the biggest reasons for people not reaching their goals is that they create direct energy challenges with the thoughts they are thinking, the words they are speaking and the actions they are taking.

When energy challenges are created

Energy challenges are created when you say one thing and do another. For example, if you say that you are going to start your own business and do nothing about it, continuing to spend all of your time on either work for an employer or non-work activities, you will probably not become self-employed. In this example, you are using the energy of thought and word as a positive energy (moving in the direction that you desire), but your actions are in direct opposition to these energies and will act as a weight to hold you back.

Another example would be to take positive action toward a goal, but in your mind continue with negative self talk. This creates restrictions.

Thinking one thing and saying another, or speaking of action and not taking any action, is like trying to drive down the road with one foot firmly placed on the gas pedal and your other foot firmly placed on the brake. You can see that you may be moving, but you are restricting yourself as to how fast you will move, and you are likely causing other problems that will ultimately manifest.

Another type of energy challenge occurs when you are working on internal positive self talk to build your image and you listen to negative words from another and allow yourself to accept those words. This creates an internal tug of war.

To stop the internal tug of war, cut off the possibility of moving backward, eliminate those self-destructive beliefs and focus on moving forward. Free yourself of old negative self talk and create new positive and supportive self talk.

Notice the energy challenges and check to ensure that your thoughts, words and actions are all in alignment. If they are not, correct and re-align in order to have all three levels of energy moving in the same direction, the direction of your desires.

Let me give you an example. Katie, one of my clients, had a goal to be at an ideal weight of 120 pounds. When she first came to me she weighed a healthy 175 pounds. With intensity, she said. "I've tried everything and nothing seems to work!" She continued, "I've joined gyms, numerous gyms, started the programs and stopped the programs. I never seem to stick to a program. I've been to all the weight loss programs, tried weight loss pills, shakes, soup diets, vegetarian diets—if there is a diet, I've tried it."

As soon as Katie began telling me her story, I knew immediately what some of her challenges were. Katie was experiencing energy challenges with her thoughts, her words and her actions at different times. It is easy in a situation like this to *say* one thing that supports your goal and *do* another that is in direct opposition to your goal—for example, express the desire to lose weight, but continue to eat foods that do not support that desire. This is Katie's story.

I got sick and tired of the way I looked. I was tired of not having any energy and looking terrible. I'd look in the mirror and be disgusted with myself, but I was doing nothing about it.

I finally decided that I had to do something. I could see how it affected the other parts of my life.

I wasn't feeling good about myself and I started treating people poorly. I became impatient, frustrated, angry and finally sad. I could see I was on a slippery slope and knew that if I didn't do something about it, not only would my health be affected, but so would my family and friends.

Katie then explained the numerous programs that she attempted in order to lose weight:

I'd be totally keen to get started. I read everything that I needed to read. If they said to do something, I did it, and I did it with enthusiasm, but in my mind I would continue with the negative self talk.

Within a week I would start to see positive results. I'd lose a few pounds.

But in my mind I could still hear the old inner voice saying, "Who do you think you are? You'll never do this."

I had an internal battle going on. I'd continue the program but my enthusiasm would drop.

The goal seemed too large and I didn't know how I would manage it. I'd look in the mirror, and even though I had lost a few pounds, I didn't look much different. I'd start to eat the wrong foods again. I'd eventually find things wrong with the "program." My commitment level would drop off and eventually I stopped completely. Then I would feel awful. I would feel like a failure. The more programs and diets I would start and stop, the worse I began to feel. I felt helpless. I felt alone. I didn't know where to turn.

She then explained how she came to me:

Inside me there was still a burning desire to lose the weight and I knew it. I'd hear myself quietly say, "Come on, you can do it." I didn't know how I was going to lose the weight, but I never lost sight of the goal.

And then a friend of mine told me about you and the work that you do with people to set and achieve goals. She explained to me that your program was not a diet program, but it was a Goal Achievement Program that was simple and easy to apply, but most importantly, got results. That's when I called you.

Katie's story is a weight loss example; however, whether it is a weight-related goal or any other goal, the same principles apply.

Katie was experiencing a number of challenges. First of all, Katie needed to be aware that she might get pushed off her path, and that would be okay, but she needed to recognize it and put herself right back on again. Human beings are habitual creatures and we condition ourselves to do and think the same things repeatedly. To change the things we think and say and do takes time. We can make the changes by repeating the necessary steps until they become habitual and second nature to us.

Katie had some great thought patterns that did support her and needed to change some that didn't support her. For example, Katie would say things like "I choose to lose weight" and "I am going to do this once and for all," and at other times, she would say things like "I'm never going to lose weight!" and "Why can't I lose weight?" These types of conflicting statements cause confusion in the brain and make energy move in one direction and then immediately move in the opposite direction.

One of Katie's great strengths was the fact that she had a burning desire to lose the weight. Without the desire she wouldn't have made it. She also decided on where she wanted to be, the end result of 120 pounds. She started to monitor her thoughts and think about what she was thinking about. I worked with her to design a program and we created her own customized goal plan.

Today Katie is happy and maintaining her weight at 122 pounds. She not only looks great physically, she feels great about herself. She has also realized that she has tremendous power within her and she can do anything she sets her mind to. She has more energy and determination than she ever imagined possible, and her self-esteem has increased immensely.

Here is a poetic story that depicts the drama of energy challenges.

The Eagle and the Wolf

There is a great battle that rages inside of me.
One side is the soaring eagle.
Everything the eagle stands for is good and true and beautiful
and it soars above the clouds.
Even though it dips down into the valleys,
it lays its eggs on the mountaintop.

The other side of me is the howling wolf
and that raging, howling wolf

represents the very worst that is inside of me.
He eats upon my downfalls and justifies himself
by his presence in the pack.

Who wins this great battle?
The one I feed!

—Author unknown

– 11 –

The Greatest Power:
BEING

Being is energy vibrating at the highest level.
Peggy McColl

—✦—

$\mathcal{M}$any books talk about achieving goals using the creative power of thought, words and deeds, but few talk about the most powerful energy available to you, the energy of **being**. When you transcend all three levels of energy—word, thought and action—through your awareness of your own states, you are into a state of **being**.

The energy of being can be demonstrated by considering your emotional states. At different times we display different emotional states. There may be occasions when one particular state of being is more predominant than another, especially when we are at the highest level of a state of being. A great example of a person being at the highest level is someone who is extremely elated. Elation is demonstrated by jumping up and down, shouting, singing, or dancing with euphoria.

We may engage in several states of being at the same time. A teacher is being nurturing, informative, reflective, focused and communicative at the time that he or she is teaching. A parent is being loving, patient, warm, kind, gentle, sweet and devoted when he or she is singing their baby a bedtime song. We choose different states of being and we choose different levels of beingness depending on our activity or the role in which we are engaged. The following is a list of some states of being.

a bringer of the light	congruent	excited
abundant	conscientious	exciting
achiever	considerate	expert
activator	courageous	faithful
adventurous	creative	fascinating
alive	creator	focused
appreciated	dedicated	friendly
appreciative	deeply in love	fully alive
attractive	deeply loved	fun
author	delightful	funny
awe-inspiring	deserving	generous
balanced	determined	gentle
bright	developer	genuine
brilliant	devoted	giving
calm	disciplined	gracious
captivating	dynamic	grateful
caring	easy-going	growing
certain	elated	happy
charismatic	elegant	harmonious
charming	empowered	healer
cheerful	empowering	healthy
classy	energetic	helpful
clever	enjoying	honest
committed	enlightened	humble
compassionate	entertaining	humorous
competent	enthusiastic	impeccable
confident	ethical	influencer

innovative	patient	spontaneous
inspired	peaceful	sporty
inspiring	phenomenal	strong
intelligent	philanthropist	successful
intuitive	physically fit	supporting
joyful	playful	supportive
knowledgeable	positive	talented
leader	professional	tenacious
lively	prosperous	tender
lovable	radiant	thoughtful
loving	relater	toned
loyal	relaxed	trusting
maximizer	respectable	trustworthy
motivated	respectful	unconditionally loving
motivating	responsible	vibrant
nurturing	results-oriented	visionary
on purpose	self-assured	vivacious
open	sensational	warm
open-minded	sensual	wealthy
organized	sexy	welcoming
outstanding	sharing	wonderful
pampered	sophisticated	worthy
passionate	spiritual	youthful

Just take one of the states of being listed above. When you are being happy your thoughts are happy thoughts, your words are happy words, you are taking the actions of a happy person and you are aware that you are happy. With all of these energies fully engaged in a state of happiness, and you are fully aware of this state of happiness, then you are *being* happy.

Do you need to be a large number of states at one time? The simple answer is no; however, you can if you choose to be. Think of the keys on a piano. There are 88 keys on a piano and each key makes its own unique sound when you press the key. In order to play a specific piece of music—for example, a piece by Mozart—you need to press certain keys in a specific sequence and with an exact tempo. To learn how to play Mozart so that it is pleasing to the ear takes time and practice, because of the many different combinations of keys and techniques being utilized.

Similarly, various roles require engaging in a number of states of being at the same time. Let's use the example of a business leader. The states of being that a business leader would engage in are dependent on a number of conditions—the type of business, the size of the business, the stage of the business (new, existing, in turmoil), his (or her) role in the business (president & CEO, vice-president, director, manager, etc.), and the length of time he has been in that position. When the business leader first became a leader, he engaged in the dominant states of being of commitment, open-mindedness, courage, focus and optimism in order to build the necessary identity of a suc-cessful business leader. Once he became a seasoned business leader, he would engage in the dominant states of being of confidence, com-mitment, faith, vision, creativity and respectfulness in order to ensure continued success. And when he was at home with his family, he would engage in the dominant states of being of unconditional love, nurtur-ing, caring, playfulness, patience and understanding to show his love and commitment to his family.

My recommendation is for you to first decide what it is that you want to have in your life (your goals) and then decide what you need to be (your states of being) in order to have that. The process of creation always starts with your states of being. In order for you to *have* some-thing, you must first *be* something.

Ask yourself questions like the following to help decide what you need to be in order to realize your goals:

In order to have a loving and fulfilling relationship in my life, what do I need to be?

In order to have a successful career, what do I need to be?

In order to have financial abundance, what do I need to be?

In order to be recognized as the best in my chosen field, what do I need to be?

(See Chapter 18 for more having/doing/being questions.)

Post your top goals

This is a tool to use to focus on your top goals and what you need to *be* in order to *have* the goal. You can do this for your priority goal, your top three goals or your top five goals.

GOALS	**BEING**
In order to have this:	**This is who/what I need to be:**
1. _____	_____
2. _____	_____
3. _____	_____

GOALS	BEING
In order to have this:	This is who/what I need to be:
1. I have my own successful business	Committed, disciplined, courageous, determined
2. I am financially independent	Knowledgeable, inquisitive, informed, skilled
3. I have a loving relationship	Loving, respectful, honest

Your states of being are your natural states. You have these states within you now. You only need to acknowledge that and demonstrate them.

Think of the dimmer switches that we talked about earlier. Your states of being are like energy switches, and to access the energy, you simply turn them on. Your thoughts, words and actions will either move the dimmer switch up or they will move the dimmer switch down, depending on how you use this energy.

If you desire to experience love in your life, notice how loving you are being. Are you thinking loving thoughts, saying loving words and behaving and acting as a loving person? If so, then you are being loving. *When we*

are being loving we are opening up ourselves to receive love. It is a short step from being loving to being loved.

If you choose to have love in your life, then think loving thoughts, say loving words and do loving things. Become aware of where your love switches are in all of those three states: when they are all turned on, you are being loving. It is a simple law of cause and effect that will operate to send love back to you, when you send it out.

Amplify the states of being

You may find that some states of being are easier for you to "turn on" than others, and other states, which you are not particularly conditioned to exercise, are more challenging to "turn on" or to "turn up."

Let's use an example. If you have a desire to be successful, and success is not a result that you have previously experienced, then being successful may be foreign to your habit patterns or conditioning.

Imagine success as a muscle that is part of you, but this muscle is one that you haven't exercised. My advice to you is to find an "expert," someone who has knowledge and experience with success and has demonstrated the use of their success muscle, or their success state of being. Ask them how they conditioned their success muscle (state of being)—how they got started, what they did first, what they did to build on the success muscle in order to be more successful. Success is a state of being that is within everyone.

Some people simply do not use this muscle, while others have developed their success muscle and continue to strengthen this muscle on a regular basis. If you haven't developed your success muscle, and your states of being are therefore weak, managing challenges and obstacles can be very difficult. When you have a conditioned state of being—in other words, when you have a powerful, fully utilized muscle—managing the challenging times becomes easier.

Sample of different energy levels

Illustration 1: In this example all of the energy levels for success are on low. The person whose energy switches are on low is not thinking of success, speaking of success, taking actions toward success. Therefore, that person is not experiencing the state of being of success.

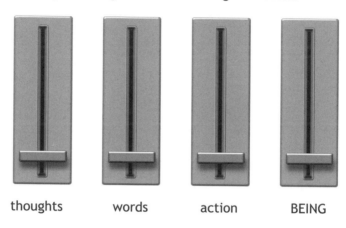

thoughts   words   action   BEING

Illustration 2: In the next example, the energy for success has started to increase for both thought and word; however, the energy of action is still low. Therefore, the state of being successful is still low.

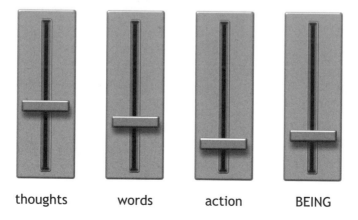

thoughts   words   action   BEING

Illustration 3: All three levels of success energy are now increasing, but still are not at their ultimate level. Therefore, the state of being reflects the combined energy levels.

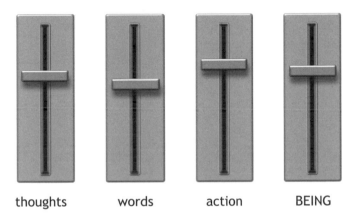

thoughts   words   action   BEING

Illustration 4: Being successful—all switches are on high. In this state you are in total awareness, with your thoughts, words and actions all being successful. Ultimately, you are in a state of being of success.

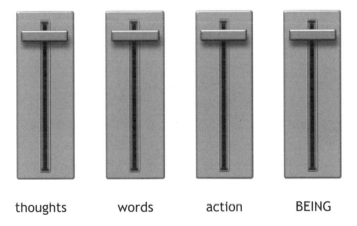

thoughts   words   action   BEING

Experiencing *being* at the highest level

All energy switches "on" is the ultimate state of being. Is it realistic to have all of your being switches on high? Absolutely! However, you may not choose to have all switches on at all times. Professional athletes demonstrate this well.

During the time that professional athletes are performing, they are at their best. If they are demonstrating states of confidence, certainty, intense focus, energy, or whatever other states they require to perform and win, during that specific time, while they are performing, they are in a total state of being. This is also known as being "in the zone." After the performance they are no longer at the high level of intensity for their performance and may move to a state of relief, gratitude, exhilaration, and maybe later on to a state of fatigue.

When I worked with two of the national Olympic teams, the primary exercise that we worked on was practicing putting themselves into the states of being of certainty, focus, faith, elation and gratitude. This process was not a one-time exercise. We worked on these exercises numerous times. The athletes invested years working on building their psychological muscles as well as on building their physical muscles.

Building your levels of being is equivalent to building your physical muscles. You cannot exercise once and expect lasting results. You must engage in exercise repeatedly. When you practice regularly, you will start to reap the rewards. It will take time.

When you have strengthened your states of being to their highest level, and you are aware that you are at the highest level, the world will begin to see the representation of your states of being. Why? Because the world will hear your words, view your actions and see your results as proof of your state of being. Our activities, behavior and outcomes will be the evidence of the states of being that we are consistently engaging in.

If you are not experiencing or do not continue to experience the goals that you desire, monitor your states of being on a regular basis. When I am coaching my clients we will monitor their states of being for a period of time and make the necessary adjustments. At the back of this book, you will find information to guide you to the States of Being Testing area on the www.onbeing.com website. You can go to this area for a guide to help you notice where your levels are each day. Clarity has tremendous power.

Being at the soul level

You can be certain that if your soul does not desire that which you *think* you want, no matter how much you focus your thoughts, speak the words, take action and try to be, you will only cause conflict in your life.

Your feelings are the expressions of your soul. Your mind experiences the past, your body experiences the present and your soul knows the future.

How do you know whether you truly desire something or not? The answer is with the tummy test. Ask yourself, "What is my gut telling me?" If you are trying to force an answer you will not get an answer.

Become quiet, very still, close your eyes and listen to your inner voice. Keep asking the question and the answer will reveal itself to you.

Or, if you are experiencing an energy challenge with your feelings expressing a desire different from what you think you desire, and you are struggling with a decision, ask yourself the question, "If I was granted one wish, at this moment, and I knew this wish would absolutely positively be granted, what outcome would I wish for?"

We all have intuitive power. Some people are more in touch with their intuition than others, but we all have this power. When you become aware of your intuitive power and start to use it, it will expand.

When your soul does not desire a goal, the reason could be because of old negative beliefs or pain that you have deeply associated with this goal. Do not try to force the process. Force negates. You can never force yourself to be something without absolute sincerity and soul's desire.

You may simply need to create new beliefs in order to no longer feel the pain. Free yourself of old pain. Consider the possibility that you may be choosing to hang on to the pain because you believe the pain protects you from experiencing further pain or greater pain in the future. If you are having trouble finding the answers within you, and you have used the techniques explained in this book, you may find it helpful to get advice from professionals, or to learn to meditate in order to let go of old beliefs, or to find release through your religious faith.

Whatever the reasons, whatever your methods, get the answers from within and choose how you will move on toward your destiny.

– 12 –

Attraction in Action

*[People] do not attract that which
they want, but that which they are.*
James Allen

———

$\mathcal{B}$earing in mind that we now understand the energy of thought, word, action and being, let us consider all of this energy in motion and the possibilities surrounding it.

Natural laws of the universe govern the creation of all things. Everything that we see around us was once an idea in the mind of another. All the inventions that we will see in the future are now simply a seed in the mind of humanity. This energy is an invisible power and we know it works because of the results that we can visibly see.

Remember that you are not the only one creating. This may help you understand why things seem to "happen" to you. If something isn't going according to your plan, it may be going according to another plan.

There are no coincidences in this world. Everything is happening according to a plan. All beings are creative, God is creative, and all that happens is according to the intentions of the creators.

Co-creation

There is tremendous power in a group of people all working toward a common goal. Why? Because you have the energy of not only one; when you add another, and then another, the resulting growth is exponential. And when you add still more, the results are staggering. This is sometimes known as co-creating. This is why it is vital in business to get all of your people working in the same direction. In my career I've worked with numerous organizations to help them understand the cost to the organization when people are not focused on the collective goals, and to help the people within the organization realize the benefits they will experience when everyone is focused in the same winning direction.

Attraction

All of creation works with the natural laws and there isn't anything that is created that is excluded from the process. Everything in the universe is vibrating because it is energy in motion. You, as a human being, are vibrating. You are vibrating in accordance with your states of being. And your states of being attract other states of being. In other words, if you are being loving, you will attract love to you. If you are being prosperous, you will attract prosperity. This is guaranteed.

Recently, a client of mine explained to me that her daughter was traveling in Australia. When her daughter called home she sounded incredibly excited. She told her mother that she was having the most amazing time of her life and that she was filled with gratitude for the wonderful people that she was meeting. Her mother told her that she was meeting wonderful people because she *is* a wonderful person. She was attracting those people into her life because of her states of being.

When you take that energy and operate/vibrate at the highest level—that is, your switch is on high—then miraculous things start to happen. There are miracles happening every day. And you are God's greatest miracle.

We have no idea of the incredible power of this energy. You can liken it to the power of a magnifying glass when it is held over a piece of paper and the sun's rays are refracted through it. You can literally burn a hole directly through the paper. This power can be intense when focused.

One of my clients had an experience with this law of attraction when he was committed to finding a new job. Bill set his mind on a specific job opportunity that was posted in the newspaper. He followed all of the steps that I suggest in my goal-achieving seminar. Bill was doing and being everything that he felt was required in order to get this job.

Bill was invited to a total of five interviews on separate occasions at the same company for a particular job. At the final stage the contest was between him and another man. Bill visualized; he created a mock-up business card with his new job title, his name and the company logo; he read his affirmations every single day. Being totally focused, he thought only those thoughts that supported his getting the job.

The end result was that the other candidate was awarded the position. At first Bill was disappointed, but then he realized that he still had the ability to find another job and he would likely find a job he would enjoy more. Rather than getting caught up in a "private pity party," he monitored his thoughts, reviewed his goals, created a revised action plan and asked himself empowering questions, starting with "What is it I would like to experience now?" and "What is great about this?"

Clearly, Bill made a conscious decision to detach himself from the outcome. As it turned out, Bill found another job that was more appropriate for his talents and skills.

Even though we intend a desired result, we must detach ourselves from the expectation of the outcome, because the Universe will provide. The Universe may not provide to you at the exact time that you would like it, but it will provide.

Do we always get what we want? Not necessarily. Why? Because creation results not only from our energy, but from that of others as well.

We may not get what we ourselves want, but we do get what the Universe wants us to have.

Recognize that in every adversity there is an opportunity. All outcomes are perfection. If the outcome was not a consciously desired outcome, convert it to something meaningful. Recognizing the meaningful outcome may be a challenge in the beginning, but have faith that you will discover the blessing as time goes on. When people do not see the opportunity in adversity, they sometimes attain a state of learned helplessness, or in other words, they feel sorry for themselves. This is a self-destructive road.

Have faith that the blessing and the perfection of adversity will reveal itself to you in time.

– 13 –

Eradicate the Poison

*E*arlier in this book there are references to the poison that kills dreams. The question asked in Chapter 5 was: "If you put poison in your water, would you drink it?" The poison referred to in that section is negative self talk and negative thoughts. Since all thoughts are energy and the energy goes out into the Universe and continues to exist forever, we really must be careful which thoughts we send out into the Universe.

The Universe is full of negativity. If you are a functioning person in this world, you are exposed to negativity every single day. Turn on the television, pick up a newspaper, listen to the radio, read a magazine, speak to a stranger on the street; everywhere we go there is poison. If there is poison everywhere, how do we avoid it?

Avoiding it is not the answer. However, you do have the option to block out negativity. Choose carefully what you are going to watch on television; read the sections of the newspaper that are not contaminated with poison; read only magazines that inspire, educate and empower you; and speak with people who are uplifting, enthusiastic and positive.

What happens when you live with a negative person? This can be a very challenging situation, but not insurmountable. The lady who cleans my home says that her husband is Mr. Negative. She has been married to this man for over 25 years. In response to the question of how to deal with this type of individual, she answered that she simply ignores him when he gets into his negative moods. She, on the other hand, is a happy and positive person. People wonder how a positive and happy person survives in that type of environment. She not only survives, but thrives, because she views her husband as a representative of the states of being to not engage in. His negativity allows her to focus on the positive side of things because she immediately notices negativity and makes a conscious decision not to engage in it. My cleaning lady is eradicating the poison, even though the poison sleeps in the same bed.

Your monitoring system

Monitor the thoughts that you allow into your mind. If you find yourself thinking negative thoughts, think again.

An exercise to build the muscle of monitoring your thoughts is to place an elastic band around your wrist. Every time you think a negative thought, snap the elastic. Within a short period of time you will likely stop thinking negative. Or you'll have a very sore wrist.

Just as you monitor your thoughts, monitor the words that you speak. Watch for excusitis. Excusitis is a disease that causes people to constantly make excuses. When you hear yourself complaining, stop immediately. Cure yourself and help cure others of excusitis. Within a reasonable period of time we should have this contagious disease under control.

Certain emotions are silent killers; they contaminate dreams. Some of these emotions are fear, stress, anxiety, anger, resentment, frustration, depression, sadness and hostility. If you are engaging in any or many of these emotions, try to determine the root cause. Do not put the lid on your problems and expect them to go away. You must deal with them.

*A blizzard creates the right conditions so
a person can build shelter from it.*
John Amagoalik

———

How do you get to the root cause? The answer is within you, but you must first have a desire to find the cause. Without desire you will not progress. If the answer to the cause of your own life's challenges is not obvious to you, then ask yourself questions that will allow the answers to surface to your conscious mind. Ask yourself, What is *really* bothering me? Or, Where did this come from? Or, How did I develop this belief? Keep asking the questions until you get the answers. The answers are within you.

Build the skills to become aware of the emotion and the cause and move to an opposite state of being.

Fear versus faith

It takes less energy to be faith-*full* than it does to be fearful. Fear is opposite to faith. Fear will immobilize you. Fear cancels out faith. You can think of fear as the breaker switch for faith. If fear is turned on, faith is automatically shut off.

People who are in a fearful state become stuck, and I call this "fear gear." If you have ever driven a car with a standard transmission you know that if you can't get the shifter into gear, you are stuck and you cannot go either forward or backward. Unfortunately, with fear, you will more likely be moving in a backward direction.

Stuck in fear gear

You can think of fear and faith on a sliding scale, the same scale. When you are being fearful you are not being faith-full. When you are exhibiting faith, there is no room for fear. Simply learn techniques to move yourself from one end of the scale to the other. You can use the techniques shared earlier in this section on choosing your thoughts, words, actions and states of being.

When people are fearful they tend to step back into safety and comfort. Is it better to step back into safety or step forward into growth? Turn that fear into power and push yourself beyond your comfort zones. This is where you will experience true growth and life at a higher level. Neale Donald Walsch taught me that "life begins at the end of my comfort zone." I've learned to turn my fear into power. Fear has not been eliminated from my life, but when it shows up, I am equipped to replace it with faith and move forward.

In my lifetime I have met people who have learned to be fearful, angry, anxious, impatient, and sometimes deeply depressed, most of the time. These individuals have invested much of their lives building the muscles of negative states of being. They have deep-rooted patterns of behavior that they repeat over and over again, which cause them to experience the same states again and again. In some ways, although they are detrimental, these states of being have served them. How could intense negative states possibly serve people? They receive attention and gain significance as a result of these states. Others will give them more attention when they are in these states of being, and they subconsciously have recognized that. As a result, they repeat the behavior. They may not even know that they are putting themselves into a negative emotion in order to receive recognition.

When I was in high school, a friend of mine was constantly sick, even though she did not have any serious illnesses. After some time she realized that she was making herself sick to get attention from her mother. The only time her mother gave her attention and love was when she was sick. When she was feeling well her mother didn't acknowledge her, but when she was sick, it was a different experience. Thankfully, she finally broke the pattern and became healthier.

If you are in a similar situation, recognize that learning to live new states of being will take discipline and will definitely take time. I believe that these learned behaviors can be overcome and that it is simple to do. It may not be easy, but it is simple.

The best way to measure your states of being is to look at your results. Your results will clearly demonstrate to you what states of being you have been consistently engaging in. If you would like to experience new results, start the cycle of creation and replace old negative energy with positive energy.

Exercise

You can use the energy switch as a gauge to determine your states of being if you would like to monitor your negative states of being. This will provide a certain level of awareness. So if you are a person who continually experiences anger, then notice the levels of anger that you are experiencing over a period of a week and use your switch several times each day, whenever you feel the anger. Move the switch up or down depending on the intensity of the anger that you are displaying. At the end of the week, replace the word "anger" with the word "calm" and start to create behavior that is calm with your thoughts, words and actions. Repeat the exercise, measuring your level of calm. Stay focused on this opposite state of being, calm, and create new behavior to support this state of being.

One of my clients completed this exercise with great success. Her personal challenge was that she was engaging in a state of anger repeatedly. Her partner had pointed out that she was always being angry. She did not believe this to be true and tried my experiment to monitor her levels of anger over a period of a week. To her amazement, her partner was revealing a part of her that she was not proud to acknowledge. Following my advice, she did not make a personal indictment against herself, but recognized the awareness as a benefit to making lasting change. She enabled herself to conduct a new exercise of consciously portraying a state of love. She set her objective to be loving and monitored her new empowering state. She has now learned to be loving as a habitual nature and has, in turn, realized phenomenal positive results.

When you are faced with making a decision in a state of stress or extreme exhaustion, you are not going to be thinking clearly. Do not make serious decisions when you are in a negative state of being—for example, stressed, impatient, tired or depressed. Be relaxed and calm when making decisions.

Stress ultimately comes from fear. And fear leads to additional challenges in your life which could possibly affect your health, relationships, finances and a number of other areas.

In life we will have challenges. How you handle them is up to you. Prepare yourself in advance for handling adversity. If you learn how to move yourself from one state of being, a negative state, to another state of being, a positive state, then you will handle adversity in a healthier way.

States of being conflicts between two people

States of being conflicts occur when there is a misinterpretation of the intentions of another.

Often I have seen conflicts between two people when one of the two believes that he or she is being loving, and their partner is not interpreting their states of being as loving.

Does this mean that the person is not being loving? Not necessarily. A possibility is that the Partner A is being loving, but Partner B is not in a loving state and therefore cannot recognize the love because he or she is vibrating at a different energy level.

Partnerships are not the only place where we experience beingness conflicts. This type of conflict occurs regularly between co-workers, between parents and their children, between teachers and their students, between coaches and their athletes, and between complete strangers.

Our states of being create filters for viewing the world. We see things differently when we are in different states. Earlier in this chapter, I talked about being in a stressful state. When you are in a stressful state, you are not seeing clearly at all. When people are in a distrustful state, they are not seeing the truth, or they may be making things up that are not even there and creating their own truth.

The chart on the following page shows two examples of states of being conflicts.

If you are experiencing a conflict, be respectful and aware of other people's states of being. Being respectful of another is not about winning someone over, or influencing the other to buy into your views; it is about understanding opposing views. The goal is awareness and not taking sides. Communication is the solution. Communicate your intention and seek to understand.

| | Partner A | | Partner B |

Engaged in the state of:	Demonstrating by:	Interprets Partner A's state as:	Filtering the actions and words as:
Playfulness, fun	Making light and humorous comments about Partner B without any thoughts of disrespect.	Mean, hurtful	Wonders if there may be some truth to the words.

| | Partner A | | Partner B |

Engaged in the state of:	Demonstrating by:	Interprets Partner A's state as:	Filtering the actions and words as:
Love	Giving their partner space and time for themselves.	Uninterested	He/she would call if they cared. Has no consideration for my feelings.

SECTION 3

On Being...

Committed

- 14 -

An Ocean of Opportunity

You are at choice always, in all ways.

—❦—

We live in a world of vast and abundant opportunities. There are opportunities everywhere. Realize that you do have the ability to create your ultimate dreams. If you have an idea, then inherent within you is the ability to create the concrete reality that idea represents. You wouldn't have had the idea if you were not able to manifest it.

There are unlimited opportunities available to you. What you will actually experience is dependent on your day-to-day choices. My son Michel plays a computer game that allows him to choose his destination and vehicle from a selection of racing trucks and a cross-selection of terrains. This game is similar to life. The game starts with choice about where you are going and how you are going to get there. As he is driving his truck along the terrain, the landscape changes depending on the direction or route that he takes. The results of all possible choices are predetermined by the game, but the outcome is based upon Michel's choices. Michel enjoys the game no matter what shows up because he detaches himself from the outcome.

This computer game has many similarities to life. Our choices determine what we will experience. All possible outcomes have already been predetermined. What we will actually experience will depend on our choices and how we react to what is happening in our lives. We should also detach ourselves from the outcome and enjoy the process because we can never be certain as to exactly what will show up.

Once you realize that there are unlimited opportunities before you, you will start to see new opportunities present themselves to you. As you become more aware, more opportunities will be presented. As you set goals and reach them, you will start to see new and grander opportunities. And it will continue. A momentum has begun. You have set in motion the process of creation.

Most people look at their own results for proof and validation. When they can validate that they were not able to create their opportunities in the past, or achieve their goals, they do not even bother to consider new possibilities.

People will also look at other people for their results and validate their decisions by other people's negative results. If you are looking for something, you will find it. If you are looking for an example to prove you can't do something, you'll get that answer. If you look for someone who has tried and failed, you will find the example.

On the other hand, if you open up your mind to new possibilities, and even though you may not have accomplished the goal in the past, you look for the example of someone who has accomplished incredible things, and you will find it.

It is important to reject the belief that if something has not been done in the past, it cannot be done in the future. If our inventors had believed that, we would not be able to communicate via multiple communications devices, we would not be able to fly across the country in a matter of a few hours, and we would certainly not be able to travel to the moon and return safely home.

Therefore, if you are in sales, do not look at last year's results to determine this year's targets. Decide where you would like to be at the end of the year. What would you like to accomplish? Set the goal and begin the work. Create a plan and follow the plan. Wayne Gretzky, one of the greatest hockey players of our time, said that he didn't look at where the puck was, he looked where he wanted the puck to go. Wayne saw his opportunities in advance.

See your opportunities in advance and use your creative energy to make them a reality.

– 15 –

Getting Clarity and Finding Your Passion

ertain unique individuals know exactly what they want in their life and they are totally committed to finding and realizing their passion. We can recognize this type of person by their results. They are enthusiastic and typically outstanding in their perform-ance and, if they are working at what they truly love, they excel in their careers.

Many people are not clear on what they want to be, do or have in their lives. That may be their choice. Not deciding in advance what you are going to be is a valid life choice. On the other hand, not choosing may be the result of not knowing how to create what you want or not knowing that you can.

If you have chosen to live your life *on purpose* and have a strong desire to live by your passion, or find your passion, then you are on the path to success.

I believe that I have found my passion in life. How do I know? There are a number of indications. First, I love what I do. I invest a consider-able amount of time and energy in what I do and it energizes me to be more, to give more. When I get up in the morning, I feel excited about what the day will bring. I think about my work all day long. On long drives I bring audio cassette programs with me and listen for hours. I don't find this to be hard work, because I love learning more about how to realize my goals and help others realize theirs. I take care of myself physically because I know that my body is the vehicle that is taking me where I choose to go. I feel very lucky to be able to do and be what I love.

Enthusiasm is at the bottom of all progress. With it there is accomplishment. Without it, there are only alibis.
Walter Chrysler

To discover what you are passionate about is a simple process. Simply think about what you love to do. Think about what gives you the most pleasure. Think about a time in your life when you were the happiest and the most peaceful and remember what it was that you were doing, having or being.

Ask the questions and you will get the answers. Be patient with this process. If you do not have answers to the questions immediately, ask again and again until you get the answers. Try different things and use your gut instinct to determine your level of passion.

Exercise

Create a passion meter, using the energy switch, and then try different things to put yourself in a passionate state, or simply think about doing different things and notice your feelings. You will be able to quickly determine your passion. Write journal notes as you go through this process to document your level of passion for different ideas.

Questions to determine your passion

You can also use the following questions to discover what you are passionate about. Record your answers as you ask the questions and review them later. Keep these questions for future reference. Your passion may

change as you get older, or your passion may change when circumstances in your life change.

You can also use these questions to determine your continued level of
passion after you have set your goals, to decide whether the goals you
have set for yourself are true for you.

What do I really want to do with my life?

What am I passionate about?

What do I love?

Where would I go if I had the freedom to go anywhere?

What would I do if I could do anything?

What would I have if there were no limits?

Who would I become?

What gives me the most satisfaction in my life?

What do I really enjoy doing in my spare time?

What motivates me?

What inspires me?

What excites me?

What drives me?

*When I have had the experience of jumping out of bed with excite-
ment, what was the cause?*

What have I done in the past that has given me the most pleasure?

How do I want to contribute to the lives of others?

What would I like to give to others?

How would I like to be remembered?

*If I were granted one wish, and I knew that that wish would be
granted, what would I wish for?*

– 16 –

Goal Setting and Goal Achieving

*Cherish your visions and your dreams as they are the children
of your soul, the blueprints of your ultimate accomplishments.*
Napoleon Hill

—❦—

hen we decide on a goal, it is usually not the goal itself that
we want, but rather the feeling we'll get when we have
achieved the goal. Ultimately, what goal setters truly strive for is a feeling, also known as a state of being.

Goal setting requires deciding in advance what it is that you would
like to experience, committing it to paper and being persistent in your
actions.

Goal setting involves making a decision about an outcome and writing
it down; this could be called "a dream with a deadline." Goal achieving
is taking that dream one step farther. Goal achieving means being committed to that dream in that you not only set the goal, you do whatever
it takes to achieve the goal, stay focused, overcome challenges, create
and follow a plan, and continually implement methods of improvement.

Desire is the starting point of all achievement. When you set a goal,
you are planting a seed. When you provide the seed with the proper
nutrition and attention, the seed will grow. Everything that is required

to manifest your goals is available to you through the energy and the natural laws of the universe.

The ability to choose is one of our greatest gifts. We have the freedom to dream, and to choose to have, be or do anything we desire. This is our birthright.

Inherent within everyone is the ability to achieve any dream we conceive, and, in order for the dream to become a reality, we must believe we can achieve it.

When you set a goal you make a decision about a dream or a desire. You are *intending* this goal into reality. Everything that is required to achieve the goal will be attracted to you when you follow the principles of goal achievement.

Locked on target

When you set a goal, your mind behaves like a missile. Once a missile is locked on a target, even if the target moves and changes direction rapidly, the missile will adjust to stay locked on the target. Similarly, when a plane is locked on autopilot, it will stay on course and automatically adjust if knocked off course.

When you set your mind on a goal, even though you may stray from your course, you will put yourself back on course and stay committed to the goal. Achieving a goal demands that you harness the power of concentration.

Set your path

We will now look at the steps to goal setting.

STEP 1: Prepare yourself to set goals

To set your goals, start out with a clean sheet of paper and ensure that you have no distractions. You will need several sheets of paper. Better yet, type your goals out on your computer.

STEP 2: Set the goal categories

Write down your goals in goal categories. Choose the categories that you would like to have for your goals. Having the categories accomplishes two things. First, it encourages you to have balance in your life, and second, it makes it easier to organize your goals.

Suggestions for goal categories are as follows:
- Career/Business
- Education
- Family
- Friends
- Finance/Savings/Income/Investments
- Home
- Personal Development (Health, Nutrition, Fitness, Skills)
- Travel
- Spiritual/Religion
- Contribution/Volunteer Work/Donations
- Things

STEP 3: Be in the highest state of being

Put yourself in a high-energy state of being, feeling great, excited and optimistic. You can achieve this high level of energy by playing your favorite upbeat music, breathing deeply, meditating, exercising briefly or whatever other activity puts you into a high state of energy.

Important to remember:
Write these goals as if you knew that you could not fail and your success was absolutely guaranteed. If you notice thoughts entering your mind like "How are you going to do that? or "You can't do that!" or any other negative thought, dismiss those thoughts and continue to dream big dreams. Use your imagination. Think of limitless opportunities and dream big.

Write out the goals as they come into your mind. Do not worry about the structure of the goal, or how you will achieve it, or the grammar; just write the goals as they come into your mind. Later in the chapter we will work on the goal statements and the steps for goal achievement.

STEP 4: Set the goals

Below are some questions that may initiate ideas or help stimulate your thought process as you go through this exercise. You can decide whether you want to use these questions or not. They are there for reference only, and to act as a guide, if needed.

What do you really want to accomplish?
- *get a degree; M.B.A., Ph.D., etc.*
- *achieve an award*
- *win a contest*
- *become a vice-president within an organization*

Who do you really want to be (become)?
- *a well-known author*
- *a TV producer*
- *a philanthropist*
- *a successful businessman/woman*
- *an executive*
- *a teacher*
- *a lawyer*
- *a medical doctor*
- *an outstanding parent*

What skills do you want to master?
- *the game of golf*
- *playing the piano*
- *being an outstanding hockey player*
- *a better time manager*

- *a great baseball player*
- *a dynamic public speaker*
- *a gourmet cook*

What do you really want to have?
- *a new car: luxury, sports, 4-wheel drive*
- *a new home*
- *a new job*
- *your own business*
- *a boat*
- *new furniture*
- *a new wardrobe*
- *your own personal trainer*
- *a cook*
- *a two-carat diamond ring*
- *a big screen TV, DVD player and surround sound*
- *landscaped property, redecorated home*

What do you want to be recognized for?
- *your contribution to society*
- *your expertise in your field*
- *your work*
- *your ability to sing*
- *your talent on the piano*
- *being in outstanding shape*
- *your investment expertise*

How do you want your family/friends/partner/customers to feel about you?
- *you are a loving, caring and helpful friend*
- *you are generous to your family*
- *you are an extraordinary business person*

- *you are an honest and ethical individual*
- *you are an extraordinary parent/stepparent*

What would you do if you knew that you could not fail?
- *climb a mountain*
- *learn to fly airplanes*
- *travel the world and travel first class*
- *go on an African lion safari*
- *build a huge custom-designed home on a lake*
- *build a resource center for holistic healing*
- *be a multi-millionaire*
- *get married to the partner of your dreams*
- *improve the level of passion with your current relationship*
- *meet a celebrity, or someone you admire*
- *be in great shape physically and emotionally*

What are the targets you want to achieve (financially, in revenue, net worth)?
- *be financially independent by the time you are x years of age*
- *exceed last year's revenue by 100 percent*
- *increase your net worth by 25 percent each year*
- *donate a minimum of 10 percent of your income to the charity of your choice*
- *have at least $10,000 cash in your bank account at any time*
- *own your home outright*
- *pay cash for your brand new automobiles*
- *have all of the money to pay for your children's university education*

STEP 5: Review the list

Take the time to review your goal list. Keep a copy with you for a period of two weeks. Add to the list as ideas come to your mind. Goals can be added and removed from your list at any time. Do not be concerned with the number of goals that you have. There is no limit to the number of goals you can have.

STEP 6: Select your top-priority goals
   Go through the initial goal list and select the top-priority goals from each category. Again, the number of priority goals is up to you. There is no predetermined number that you need to select.

STEP 7: Set the timeframe for achievement
   Once you have selected the top-priority goals, you will now identify the timeframe for achievement. In other words, when would you like these goals to be realized? Some goals may be "ongoing" and you can label them as such.

Is it a goal or not?

There are no hard and fast rules about what a goal is or is not. If there is something you want to have, do or be in your life, then it is a goal. Goals do not only refer to material items. Goals can also be characteristics or personality traits. If it is something you want and you do not presently have, then it is a goal.
   A goal may also be something that you currently have and you want to continue to have; therefore, you have made it a goal because it is a priority. For example, if you currently have a very loving, passionate, honest, fun, caring, committed relationship with your life partner and it is something that is vitally important to you, then you may choose to have this as a written goal.

STEP 8: Write out goal statements for your goals
   Goal statements are powerful statements. Repeating a goal statement over and over again, with conviction and sincerity, will start to build belief systems.
   Goal statements use the power of *thought*, one level of creative

energy, and the power of *word*, another level of creative energy. When you consistently affirm a statement, it is only a matter of time before the energy moves into form.

Note:

When writing your goal statements, use the words "I am" or "I have" and do not use the words "I want." Why? Because "I am" and "I have" are declarations of your choice. The subconscious mind does not distinguish between what is real and what is vividly imagined. When you use the words "I want," the universe will respond and provide you with the experience of wanting the goal, not having the goal. Wanting something is always placing it in front of you and not claiming the goal to be a choice.

Below are the guidelines to be followed when creating your goal statements. Ensure each and every goal statement follows these guidelines:

1. Write your goals in the present tense, as if you have already achieved the goal, using "I am" and "I have."

2. State your goals in the positive and choose your words carefully. Your mind will trigger on certain words. For example, if your goal is weight-related, ensure that you write out your ideal weight and use words such as "slim," "ideal weight," "healthy," and do not use words such as "fat," "heavy" or "overweight."

3. Use "ing" verbs in your statement wherever you can (driving, enjoying, celebrating, flying, cruising, singing, etc.) For example; "I [your name] am proudly receiving the Award for..." Verbs in the present tense will help you experience the feelings that you will have when you achieve this goal.

4. When writing out your goal statement, state your full name. For example, "I, Joe Smith, am gratefully enjoying being an example of outstanding contribution to..."

5. Ensure the list of your top goals is written in your own handwriting, typewritten or computer-printed, and clearly displayed.

6. When writing out your goal statement, be specific and clearly define your goal (if you are clear about the result you desire).

GOAL STATEMENT EXAMPLES

I, John Doe, am enjoying driving my brand new convertible BMW 535i.

I, Jane Smith, am enjoying being at my ideal weight of 115 lbs. I am fit and in excellent shape. I love to exercise and I do so on a regular basis.

I, Bob Jones, am having a wonderful time on the Caribbean cruise with my new bride on our honeymoon. I have gratefully met and married the woman of my dreams. She is extraordinary and we love each other unconditionally. We treat each other with respect and honesty.

I, Mary Smith, am happily enjoying the spectacular view from the window of our beautiful cottage on a clear and clean lake.

I, John Doe, am happily enjoying running my profitable and successful business. I offer tremendous value to my customers, and as a result, they benefit from the use of our products. Our revenue this year has exceeded last year's numbers by 200 percent.

I, Bob Doe, am enjoying cutting our beautiful landscaped lawn with my brand new ride-on lawnmower.

I, Jane Smith, have gratefully paid for my home with cash. I now own my home outright. It feels great to know that I am absolutely financially free.

I, Brenda Jane, am enjoying the feeling of exhilaration after accomplishing my goal of earning my M.B.A.

STEP 9: Read your goal statements
Read your goal statements at least twice a day, every day. The best time to read your goals is just before you go to sleep. It is at this time that your conscious and subconscious mind are most receptive. This allows the subconscious mind to accept what you have written as a reality.

Take the opportunity to read your goals throughout the day. If you are sitting in traffic, take out your goals and read them. If you are waiting at the dentist's office, read your goals while you wait. If you are watching television, keep your goals handy, and read them during the commercials. Carry your goals with you wherever you go.

Share your goals only with people who will support you. If you think people will not support you and your goals, do not share your goals with them. This is important because it will allow you to avoid any negative input or possible non-empowering thoughts entering your mind.

If people will support you, share your goals. You may find these people to be great support and they may also intensify the energy.

When reading your goals, say them out loud and say them with conviction. The intensity will contribute toward building the beliefs and putting energy in motion, as described earlier in the book.

STEP 10: Monthly activities for goal achieving:
Every month, review your goals and monitor your progress. Here is a handy checklist for monthly activities:

- Set monthly goals as stepping stones to reach your larger goals.
- Measure and monitor your progress.
- Measure and monitor your states of being.
- Practice engaging in the states of being that support your goals. Be the source of these states to others.

- Create a plan to achieve your goals.
- Follow the plan you have set for your goal achieving.
- Create a contingency plan or backup plan.
- If your results are not the results that you desire, try something else.
- Enter action items into your daily schedule or time-management system.
- Visualize yourself already in possession of your goals.
- Feel what it will feel like when you achieve your goals.
- Decide how you will celebrate when you achieve your goals.
- Establish your daily code of conduct (disciplines) and follow it.
- Stay focused on your goals in everything that you do.
- Ask yourself empowering questions.
- Keep an Accomplishment file and enter the goals once you achieve them. Add thank you cards and your favorite sayings. Review this file from time to time.
- Be grateful for the gifts in your life and the gifts that you are creating.
- Acknowledge another for the gifts that they bring to your life.

– 17 –

Creating Lasting Change

*The greatest discovery is that human beings can
alter their lives by altering their attitudes of mind.*
William James

—✦—

reating lasting change requires an investment of time and energy. Keep putting in great thoughts, reading from great books, listening to inspirational audio programs, attending seminars and speaking with supportive people. Practice doing and being all of the things that are necessary to create the changes you desire in your life, and you will reap the rewards. This process does take time.

One of my own challenges has been that I want things now. I have learned the hard way that forcing does not work. Actually, force negates. When I reach a point of "wanting" a goal to manifest itself in form earlier than the process of creation will allow, I remind myself to be patient and trust in the creation process. This is a simple example of practicing what I preach, as outlined in this book.

Notice the strategies that work best for you. Everyone is different; we are all unique beings. You will find your own uniqueness in the process. The amount of time that it takes for one person to achieve their goals can be dramatically different from the time it takes for another person.

Remain true to yourself. But remember, what is true for you can change over time. Something may be true for you today and several years down the road, the same fact is no longer true. Why? Because you have created new perspectives and new beliefs.

Know that you are in an evolving process. You can think of starting with a new recipe to get a new result, a beautiful result. If you have ever made something from a recipe you know that all of the ingredients are important to create the result you are working toward. You first decide what it is that you want to bake or cook. You follow with a plan to produce the result, determining what you need as ingredients, knowing the quantities and sequence.

Leaving out any of the ingredients can completely change the end result. You will, in fact, get a result, but it may not be the result you intended. Leaving out an ingredient or a combination of ingredients, or the main ingredient, will definitely affect the final product.

The next time you go to play a game of golf, decide in advance what kind of a game you are going to have. I've played golf with golfers who would say, as we were approaching the course, "I'm going to have a terrible game today." I would ask them, "Is this what you have decided to experience today?" Invariably they would laugh and realize what they were saying and doing.

Focus

When I was a little girl in grade school my teachers would consistently write in my report card, "Peggy is easily distracted." I was a very curious person and noticed everything that was going on around me.

Curiosity has its place. But distraction in a classroom, at inappropriate times, can lead to poor grades. Being curious created challenges going through school, and in order to apply myself to my work, I had to develop techniques to get and stay focused. For example, I would keep my head down if I was working on an assignment and intentionally not lift my head when I heard a distracting sound. When the teacher was speaking, I intently focused all of my attention on him or her and did not move my eyes from them. These practices took time to develop into habitual behavior, but over a period of time, my grades improved dramatically.

The movie *For the Love of the Game* with Kevin Costner shows an example of applying focus. Kevin portrays the role of a professional baseball player, specifically, the pitcher on the team. In one scene in the movie, Kevin needs to block out the noise of the crowd and, in order to do this, he uses a technique called "clear the mechanism." In his mind he blocks out all of the noise and focuses on the delivery of his pitch. His mind becomes quiet even though there is an incredible amount of noise around him.

Getting focused or increasing your focus requires getting your thoughts, words, body, actions and emotions in alignment in a specific direction. Make a decision on what you need to be doing and/or being at a specific time: do it and be it. If you find yourself getting distracted, put yourself back on track.

When you are driving a car along a highway, you must keep focused on where you are going. You may take your eye off the road for a second, but if you do not return your focus to driving, you will have challenges!

Focus is not a state that you need to engage in 100 percent of your time. Apply focus when you need to apply focus. As I was writing this book, there were certain days that I decided I would focus only on writing and content. When I neared the completion of the book, I created a schedule for the final month and utilized my focus skills to maintain my focus during this period of time.

Creating the schedule was a tool that I developed to keep my focus. Placing the schedule in front of my desk, in order to have it in full view, was another method of keeping my focus. Some days I felt like going out of the office, or taking a walk, but I did not allow myself to take my eye off the goal. Every day I worked on keeping my focus.

Create a reward system for small successes. As I wrote the book, I would allow myself to take breaks after I had completed an idea, paragraph, page or chapter. I would separate the project into chunks and set goals and small rewards for each chunk. At the conclusion of the project I booked a celebration dinner. If I found myself losing focus as I worked on the project, I would think of the contribution the book would make to others, and the rewards for myself and others, and push myself a little harder to get right back on track. One technique is to imagine a hand on your back that gives you that little extra push when you need it.

- *18* -

Questions to Enhance and Increase Focus

*W*hen you ask yourself a question, or someone asks a question of you, your attention immediately shifts to the subject of the question. There are questions that build and support your dreams and there are questions that destroy and undermine your dreams.

Become aware of the questions that you are asking yourself and notice if they are supportive questions or questions that are destroyers of dreams. Notice the energy or attention that you are giving to other people's questions, and again ask yourself: are these supportive questions or questions that destroy dreams? At that point, you can decide whether you will give the question additional thought and/or energy.

One evening, while I was writing this book, I received a telephone call from a gentleman who was selling calendars on behalf of Harvest House Ministries. Harvest House is a therapeutic community that serves drop-outs from other programs, people in jail, people who live in the streets and people who want treatment. They offer a drug and alcohol treatment program to help people deal with chemical dependency. The name of the young man who called was Rico.

Rico was 13 when he starting abusing substances. For 13 years (between the ages of 13 and 26) he created a terrible life for himself and for those with whom he came in contact. He was on a downward spiral. Even though Rico came from a family of successful people, he made different choices for his life, a life that turned to crime. Ultimately, Rico could not hold on to a job. He was in and out of prison. When he went to prison, he thought that his addictions would be dealt with, but they were not. In prison, he learned only how to survive in prison.

At the young age of 26, when Rico felt there was no more hope, he was introduced to Harvest House. Harvest House was not the first treatment center or treatment method that he tried. He had attempted treatments through Alcoholics Anonymous, Narcotics Anonymous, Cocaine Anonymous, the Salvation Army and numerous others, but to no avail.

Within every misfortune there is a seed of greatness. At Harvest House, Rico found what he needed to turn his life around. It started with desire. Rico had a very strong desire to make changes to his life and he knew that he had to do it and nobody else was going to do it for him. Rico has recently been reunited with his family and has been accepted into law school. He continues to reside at Harvest House and helps support the program by running the fundraising department.

What does Rico's story have to do with questions? When Rico was sharing his compelling story with me on the telephone, he talked about the questions he would ask himself after he got out of jail. He had not dealt with his drug addictions and every day he asked himself questions like "How will I get cocaine today?" Not "will I...," but "how will I?" The difference is in the determination. He decided he would get cocaine and all he had to figure out was the "how." These were the types of questions that Rico would ask himself repeatedly, increasing his desire to get the drugs.

Now that he is in Harvest House, he told me, he notices that he asks himself different types of questions. For example, when he awakes in the morning, he asks himself, "How will I contribute today?" Or "How will I help others today?" You can see that Rico has used the power of questions to focus on his desired results. It is not only Rico who realizes the benefits, but also the many others that he has the privilege to help.

The following are examples of questions that you might consider selecting for your daily questions. Choose questions that you can ask yourself in the morning to set the right direction for your day.

Goal setting and decision making

What do I really want to accomplish?
Who do I really want to be (become)?
What skills do I want to master?
What do I really want to have?
What do I want to be recognized for?
How do I want my family/friends/partner/customers to feel about me?
What would I do if I knew that I could not fail?
What are the targets I want to achieve (financially, in revenue, net worth)?
What would I like to experience in my life?
What do I choose to experience in my life?
What do I want to have, do or be?
What decisions do I need to make today toward the achievement of my goals?
What choices will I make today toward the attainment of my goals?

Goal achieving and focus

What actions will I undertake today that will take me in the direction of my goals?
Where do I choose to focus my consistent thoughts?
What will I visualize today that supports my goals?
How will I increase my level of focus?
What disciplines will I now engage in that will help support me in the achievement of my goals?

Handling adversity and overcoming challenges

What is great about this?

What would a loving person do now?

What else could this mean (answer in a positive way)?

What will I remember about this event that will help me in the future?

What can I do right now to make this better?

What will I focus on right now to help me feel better about this?

How can I use this to benefit myself and others?

What is the blessing in this?

Being

Is this who I choose to be?

Who am I?

Is this who I am?

What can I be for you?

What will I do now to demonstrate the highest level of my states of being?

As I am an unconditionally loving being, what will I do now?

How can I demonstrate the highest aspect of who I am?

How will I give to others to make a positive difference in their lives?

How will I help others achieve their goals?

What am I committed to being today that will take me in the direction of my goals?

How will I demonstrate my highest level of being loving right now?

What kind of day would I like to experience today? What do I need to be in order to have that kind of day?

For what am I most grateful?

How will I make this day a masterpiece?

Having/doing and being

In order to have a loving and fulfilling relationship in my life, what do I need to be?

In order to have a successful career, what do I need to be?

In order to have financial abundance, what do I need to be?

In order to be recognized as the best in my chosen field, what do I need to be?

In order to have great grades in school, what do I need to be?

In order to have increased sales, what do I need to be?

In order to know that I am contributing at the highest level, what do I need to be?

In order to have a well toned and healthy body, what do I need to be?

In order to have balance in my life, what do I need to be?

In order to be an outstanding parent, what do I need to be?

In order to have wonderful and meaningful friends, what do I need to be?

In order to have a luxurious and opulent lifestyle, what do I need to be?

In order to have peace with who I am, what do I need to be?

In order to live my life on purpose, what do I need to be?

– 19 –

Faith

Faith can move mountains. When faith is applied to your goals it gives creative energy increased intensity.

Every living thing has faith in something or someone. You may have had faith in something you knew for certain was true and you experienced exactly what you believed in, and that again confirmed your faith.

Remember a time when you had faith and it served you well. Live these experiences again in your mind until you can really feel in touch with the feeling of faith. Apply this state of faith to something that you desire and keep practicing. Whether you have faith or not is your choice.

Faith can be built over time. If you have little faith today, be grateful for the faith that you have. Add to this faith by practicing being trusting. Create a faith energy switch and monitor your level of faith. Once you become aware of your level of faith, and you consciously decide to increase the level of faith, as it relates to your goals, then practice being trusting, or faith-full, every single day. Have faith in God or the Universe to support your goals. Have faith in yourself and your own ability to reach your goals. Do the things that support having faith by continually staying focused and taking action. Your effort in taking action will also help build your faith.

Never underestimate the power of faith. Faith alone has miraculous power to achieve your goals.

> *Now faith is the substance of things hoped for,*
> *the evidence of things not seen.*
> Hebrews 11:1

Building the Beliefs

Remember as you are striving to create new results in your life that, along with having faith, you must build the supporting beliefs. Create the new beliefs that support your goals and create the necessary identity of the new you. You may want to look back at Chapter 8 to review building beliefs.

When your new beliefs are created, you will start to see things differently and experience things differently. Continue to build, with a commitment to the process.

This step in the process of goal achievement cannot be bypassed. Without it you are certain to return to your old patterns of behavior. Build the beliefs with affirmations. Create a goal chart for your top goals. This goal chart will give you everything you need to create the beliefs.

Goal Charts

A goal chart will help you stay focused on a specific goal. A goal chart encapsulates the creative process on one page by articulating a goal (Have), thoughts, words, actions (Do), and the states of being (Be) you require to engage in consistently to realize the goal.

Place your goal chart in a location where you can see it regularly. Post it on your refrigerator or your bathroom mirror. Read it every day. Create goal charts for your top goals.

The following is an example of a blank goal chart:

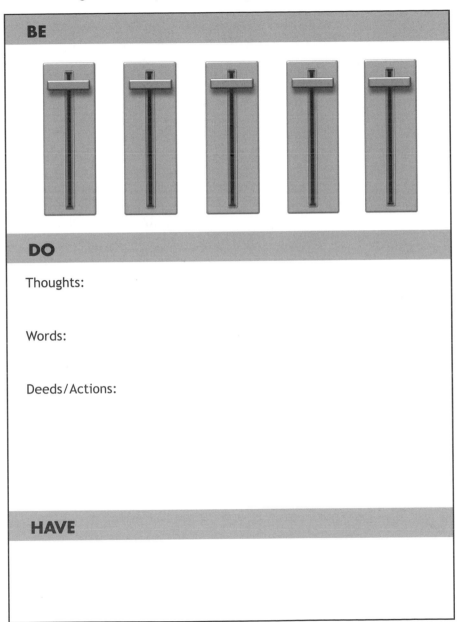

The following is an example of a completed goal chart:

BE

| Confident | Dedicated | Faithful | Focused | Grateful |

DO

Thoughts: I am committed to follow through. I am focused on my goal in everything that I do. I have faith in myself.

Words: I am joyfully flying my beautiful brand new airplane. I have made my dream come true. I knew that I could do it. I am constantly finding new ways of earning additional income. I am an outstanding saver. I am thrilled with seeing the balance in my savings account rise at a phenomenal rate.

Deeds/Actions: Open up a separate account for my airplane fund. Transfer funds to start to build the account. Make deposits to this account each month based on a minimum of 10 percent of earned income.

HAVE

I, Bob Smith, am enjoying flying my brand new Cessna C172M 4-seater floater airplane.

– 20 –

Visualization

If one advances confidently in the direction of their dreams,
and endeavors to live a life which they have imagined,
they will meet with a success unexpected in common hours.
Henry David Thoreau

—✦—

$\mathcal{W}$hen you have a goal similar to Bob Smith's goal in the previous chapter, to have an airplane, the visualization becomes easy. Athletes are taught to continually visualize their performance, including every tiny detail. Studies show that visualization can bring about an increase in results by as much as 75 percent.

When you visualize, you experience the feelings associated with achieving your goal in your body. This contributes to building the supportive thoughts, words, actions and states of being.

Train yourself to deliberately picture your desire and carefully examine the picture. Associate yourself fully with all of the images that are created in the full visualization exercise. Shakti Gawain wrote a wonderful book on the subject of visualization entitled *Creative Visualization*. I suggest you not only buy it and read it, but study it and do the exercises in the book.

Effective visualization exercises create vibrations that work according to the Law of Attraction.

You can do visualization exercises anywhere. Visualization is an easy process to incorporate into your daily routine. Relax before doing the visualization, but you do not have to close your eyes to perform visualization. You can visualize—also known as imagining—as you drive down the road. So, if you spend a considerable amount of time each day in an automobile, visualize while you are driving.

You can also visualize while you are waiting for a meeting, waiting to pick someone up, standing in line at the grocery store, sitting at a traffic light, or sitting in the parking lot before getting out of your car.

For best results, determine a period during the day when you can most effectively do the visualization exercise. Relax your body and your mind. Close your eyes and start to imagine yourself already in possession of the goal. See yourself enjoying the results. See the benefits that others will enjoy. Expand your thoughts to create a vivid picture. Feel the feelings and enjoy the exercise.

My house story

This particular story is my own story. Several years ago my husband Charles and I decided our relationship was going to change form. We chose to no longer cohabit and we chose to be great friends for the benefit of our beautiful son Michel and for our own benefit. To this day, Charles is one of my most cherished friends. Our relationship now, as a divorced couple, is incredibly healthy. As a result, Michel has not been negatively affected by our parting of ways.

Once Charles and I made the decision to divorce we put our home up for sale. At that time the real estate market was poor. Also, we were living on an acre in the country, and country living only attracted a certain kind of buyer. In the two years that we had our house up for sale we did not have one serious offer. Charles and I agreed that he would keep the home and I would find a new home in another location.

There was only one problem. I didn't have any money. The value of the house that Charles and I owned had decreased in value and Charles was in fact doing me a favor by releasing me from the house and the mortgage.

I set my goal to own and live in a four-bedroom home, detached, with three bathrooms and a double-car garage, in a modern subdivision with lots of trails and parks around where Michel and I could go cycling. At the time I set the goal I had no idea where the house would be and I had no idea how I would pay for it. I simply decided what I wanted to experience.

I started looking at houses, going to open houses and new home show-rooms. Charles would say to me, "Peggy, why are you bothering to look for a house when you don't have any money? Why don't you get an apartment?" But I was adamant that I would own a home and I would not consider any other option.

While I was in the process of looking for a home I heard of an inter-esting lottery in our city. It was called "The Dream of a Lifetime." The way it worked was that you could buy a ticket for $100, giving you the opportunity to win a grand prize. One of the prizes was a large home that was completely furnished, professionally decorated, professionally landscaped, complete with two new cars, groceries, legal costs, moving expenses, and cleaning services for one year.

When I heard of this draw, I said "Perfect!" This *was* perfect for me. It would be a great solution to my situation.

The Dream Home, as they called it, was open during the day for vis-iting. I drove out to the home, passing several parks and nature trails, and arrived at a beautifully decorated, four-bedroom, three-bathroom, detached home with a double garage, located in a nice modern subdi-vision.

I walked in the front door and immediately started visualizing. I sat in all of the rooms and visualized. There was a lady house-sitting and I sat with her at the kitchen table and I imagined that she had come to visit me. I would look out the window and see Christmas lights on the neigh-bors' trees and say to myself, "This is what it will be like at Christmastime when I live here." Upstairs I went through all the rooms. I decided which bedroom would be Michel's. I would lie on the large bed in the master bedroom and visualize. I got in the bathtub and imagined having a wonderful warm bubble bath in my great Roman tub. I would vividly imagine all the details and smell the scents of the bath oils. I kept my clothes on for the bathtub exercise, but the effect was the same!

Several times I would visit the house and visualize living in it with my son Michel. I would walk down the street. I would drive to the house and imagine coming home from work. I changed my goal card to say *"I, Peggy McColl, am enjoying living in my four-bedroom, three-bathroom, impeccably decorated home, fully furnished with the finest quality of furniture, and with a double-car garage, at 71 Stonemeadow Drive in Kanata."*

On December 7, the Dream of a Lifetime draw was held and a doctor from the hospital won the house.

What did I do? I changed my goal card and simply eliminated the address. I did not lose sight of my goal.

Several months passed and I was visiting my brother Bob and my sister-in-law Alice at their cottage. In the middle of the night, I awoke and sat bolt upright. I felt a strong *message* being delivered. It was extremely odd, although I didn't think of it as odd at the time. The message was "go to the house." I immediately knew that the message meant to go to the house in Kanata, the Dream Home at 71 Stonemeadow Drive.

The next day we left Bob and Alice's cottage and headed for home. Michel and my nephew James were with me and I told them that I needed to take a small detour. I drove over to the house at 71 Stonemeadow Drive, and as we drove up to the house I noticed a for sale sign on the lawn. I knew that this was indeed a *sign*.

Keep in mind I still didn't have any money, but something inside me told me that I needed to get back in this house. The next evening I went to visit my friends Marin and Anick, who happened to live in the same neighborhood. I told them that I was going to call the real estate agent and go and visit the house. Marin quickly responded with, "What for?

Why would you drag a real estate agent out of his home on a cold winter's night to show you a house that you are very familiar with, and besides, you don't have any money and that house is a quarter of a million dollars?" I replied, "The real estate agent doesn't know that I've been in the house and he certainly doesn't know what my financial situation is." With that, I called the agent.

A short time later Anick and I were visiting the home with the real estate agent. The moment I walked in the door I started my visualization exercises again, only this time I turned up the intensity.

During the week that followed I visited the house again with the real estate agent two additional times. I drove by the home every single day. On the Friday of that week, I was driving by and I was listening to motivational tapes on my tape deck, as I always do. This time it was Tony Robbins speaking to me. He was talking about "The philosophy of stretching." He said "The philosophy of stretching is when you think you can't, you must. Not for what you'll get but for what you'll become." I knew Tony was talking to me.

I reached for my cellular telephone and called the agent. I said, "Geoff, I want to make an offer." He met me at the house and we sat at the kitchen table. I came up with this idea: to move into the house in May, give the seller 10 percent of the purchase price on the day I moved in, occupy the house for six months, and close on December 1st. Geoff had never heard of such a thing, but he felt compelled to make the offer.

After a brief negotiation I had a deal. I bought a house without any money, but I knew that I would follow through. I had complete faith in myself and I had complete faith in the Universe.

In order to give the offer, I had to do a credit card transfer to have the cash to cover the deposit check. I did not share my actions with anyone. If I had told people what I was doing they would have likely said "You're crazy." I took a huge leap of faith, but I knew that I had to follow through because now I had made a commitment.

I managed to raise the money for the move-in date in May, as a result of a suggestion from my friend Val. However, I was still faced with the challenge of raising enough money to close the deal on December 1st.

Fortunately, my employer at the time was a new Internet company that was about to go public. Going public was a new experience for me, as was the Internet. Many people were not even aware of what the Internet was at that time. I had decided that I would take all of the money that I had saved for the house closing (which wasn't enough to close) and put it on the IPO (Initial Public Offering). This was a huge gamble and a huge risk.

The IPO was originally set for October, which would provide me with a two-month window. However, the date became a moving target and was continually delayed. Finally, four days before my house was closing, the IPO was set to go. I put all my money on the stock, and within 24 hours I had earned all of the money that I needed to close the deal.

Was I nervous? You bet. Did I have doubt? Certainly, but I refused to give up. I was absolutely certain of my ability and I transferred that certainty to knowing that I would complete this transaction.

In no way am I suggesting that you go out and buy a house without any money. I'm not saying that you can't do that, but there are a few fundamentals to consider. Personally, I had a number of things going for me. I knew how to clearly define my goals. I understood the creative energy of the Universe; I had faith in that and I had faith in myself. I also knew my level of commitment and perseverance. I knew I would do what it took to follow through.

There isn't a day that goes by that I'm not grateful for that experience. I grew more in those six months than I had in the previous six years. It is true what Tony was saying about stretching: "It isn't for what you'll get, it is what you'll become." I developed new empowering states of being and, to this day, they constantly serve me and, in turn, help me to help others.

– 21 –

Monitor Your Progress and Notice the Results

*A*s you progress on the road to goal achievement, look at the results you are getting and evaluate the results.

If you are not getting any results, there may be a number of reasons for it. Do not immediately assume that the goal is unattainable. There could be a simple answer. You may be on the brink of a breakthrough. You may have to take one more step, or rely on the universal energy to respond to your intention. If you have the desire, stick with your commitment.

As a tool to evaluate your progress and your results, use questions. Questions will open up your mind to new possibilities and new opportunities.

Consider the following questions:

Did I break down the goal into baby steps or smaller goals and create milestones to reach the larger goal?

Am I missing something that is obvious and I haven't taken the time to reflect or evaluate the action steps that I am taking?

Am I taking the wrong route? Is there a better way?

Have I considered all of the options?

Should I consider changing directions or trying another approach?

Have I been watching all the signs along the way?

Have I been returning to old conditioning and moving backward instead of forward?

Have I created a plan that is solid enough? Or, do I need to review my plan and make changes?

Am I taking the long road; is there a better route?

Am I totally off track?

What resources can I use to help me with achieving this goal?

Who can help me to achieve this goal?

What tools will I use to help me achieve this goal?

Is this taking me in the direction of my goal or farther away?

What do I now need to do (be) in order to reach my desired result?

How will I know if I am getting the right results? (This question will allow you to anticipate the results in advance.)

Re-evaluating the goals you have set

If you set a goal and made it a priority, and you haven't yet taken action, you may want to revisit the goal. Ask yourself if you truly have a desire to have this goal. If you do have a desire, then there may be a blockage that needs to be discovered and removed.

Review your goals on a regular basis. At least twice a year, go through the step-by-step exercises of goal setting as illustrated in Chapter 16 of this book.

Goal lists

It is advisable to keep a file of all of your goals, and place your top-priority goals, written as goal statements, in an accessible place to view every morning and every evening. Also keep a written copy of the top-priority goals with you at all times.

As you achieve your goal, write the word VICTORY in large letters across the goal and place it in a file labeled "Accomplishments." Review this file from time to time. You will feel good looking back over the goals that you have set and achieved. An accomplishment file is a great resource to have on hand when you need a boost or some inspiration.

SECTION 4

On Being...
An Achiever

- 22 -

Building Confidence

Confidence is an inside job. You will not get confidence from something outside of yourself. If you seek to gain confidence from a job or a relationship or from some other source, you are setting yourself up for disappointment.

I've seen extremely talented people become insecure when they lost their job, because they had tied their confidence level to their career. I've seen athletes leave their profession as athletes and become bums in the street because they had all of their confidence tied up in their athletic ability and their athletic performance.

*If you have no confidence in self, you are twice
defeated in the race of life. With confidence, you have
won even before you have started.*
Marcus Garvey

If you want to have confidence, then be confident. Being confident is believing in yourself, believing in your own inner power and your own inner strength. Being confident is possible for everyone. We were all born with the ability to be any state of being we desire. There is no select group of states of being designed for certain people. You may know of an individual who has specific states of being that are particularly attractive to you, or they have states of being that you would like to have: you have the ability to have those states of being too! There are no limits to the states of being that you can have, except those limits that you acknowledge. We have seen this before, in other chapters.

So, if confidence is something that you strive for, then be confident. Here are some strategies to build confidence:

- Make decisions when decisions need to be made
- Stick to the decisions that you make
- Be true to your word
- When you make a commitment, follow through
- Keep a record of your accomplishments
- List your greatest assets
- Focus on the skills you would like to build and get on with the work
- Set goals
- Take steps toward the achievement of your goals
- Be honest with yourself and with others
- Be loving with everyone you meet
- Give unconditionally
- Give abundantly

- When asked to do something, go the extra mile

When a person is confident you can see it. They walk as if they are confident, they perform with confidence, and their results are superior because of their level of confidence.

Being insecure is not a fun place to be. If you are experiencing insecurity in any area of your life, seek to move your meter up to the state of confidence. You can accomplish this in a relatively short period of time by following the suggestions and guidelines in this chapter and in this book.

– 23 –

Knowing

*W*hen you are working toward a goal, one of the states that you will benefit from is the state of absolute certainty, the state also known as *knowing*. Knowing is the state in which you have surpassed wishing, hoping or believing. Knowing is the anchor state for belief. When you are in a state of knowing and you stay there, you can accomplish great things. Your commitment and your level of focus become easy. Handling adversity and overcoming obstacles and challenges is a breeze. You become unstoppable. This is a wonderful place to be.

Knowing is also a gut-level instinctual feeling. Knowing is your soul revealing itself to you. Therefore, you can create a state of knowing for the achievement of a goal and you can draw out a state of knowing from deep within.

Have you ever experienced a situation where you just knew something was true? You may not have had any evidence, but you *knew* it to be true.

This story is about a client I worked with a couple of years ago. This particular client, whom we'll call Linda, was married for 22 years and had three teenaged boys. Her husband had a job that required him to travel extensively. When I met Linda she was ready to leave her husband and create a new life for herself. When I inquired into the reason, she simply replied that she knew that he was having an affair. Up until the point that she finally confronted her husband, she had no proof, she had not previously asked him, she did not hear this from another; she just knew. In her heart, in her soul, she knew.

Linda and her husband had a calm and easygoing relationship. They met when they were in high school and married at a young age. Throughout their marriage they experienced ups and downs, but for the most part, there was nothing that they didn't overcome. Their marriage had never been in jeopardy during the period of time they were together. She had truly believed that they were going to be together forever.

Then, a few years before she spoke to me, she started to get these feelings about her husband. She immediately dismissed them, thinking she was being ridiculous. She was not a jealous person and her husband was far from flirtatious. She didn't have any evidence and her husband appeared to be behaving exactly the same as ever. But the feelings continued. She said it was like a voice inside of her that had started to scream, "Wake up! Your husband is having an affair."

Linda did not want to confront her husband because she thought that, if she did confront him, he would think she didn't trust him, and her belief was that marriage was built on trust. But the feelings became so intense, she said, that she had a complete knowing of his affair to be true. The entire time that she was experiencing these feelings, she never saw any clear evidence.

When Linda finally asked her husband if her *knowing* was true, he admitted his infidelity. Linda had spent two years thinking about the ramifications of the possibility that he was having an affair. She thought about the hurt she would feel, and got totally in touch with those feelings. She thought about what she would do and how they would arrange their schedule with the boys. She thought about where they would live. She went through the entire process for two years, so that when she actually got to the event, the separation, she was prepared mentally and emotionally.

The separation for Linda was extremely difficult. She valued the sacredness of a marriage union and she believed that their marriage was no longer the type of relationship in which she wanted to be involved.

Calmly and gently, Linda and her husband planned the separation. Today, Linda is at peace with her new life. She has arranged her life to suit her new situation, and now spends quality time with her three boys. She runs a home business that allows her to continue to take care of the things that are most important to her, her family.

Linda had a knowing. Where did this knowing come from? Knowing comes from getting in touch with the universal energy. Knowing is increased when we intuitively feel the power of our own energy, the energy of another, or the energy of a group of others.

Understanding this can also allow us to *create* a state of knowing. How? We can build a state of knowing by using our own energy and continuously guiding it in a specific direction, and repeating the process for a period of time. Start with the sense of knowing that you begin to feel. Do not allow a negative emotion, such as fear, to lead you away from a state of knowing. Continue to allow this energy to flow and allow the messages that you are receiving, via your feelings, to come into your awareness. These messages and/or feelings are the confirmation of your knowing. In this way, knowing can be developed.

As we mentioned earlier, your feelings are the expressions of your soul. It is your soul's way of speaking to you. This is also where your intuition derives.

If there is something that you need answers to, then get quiet, calm your mind, relax your body and listen to your body. Meditating is often an effective method to tap into your knowing (your soul).

Another client of mine, who was experiencing intense relationship trauma, once asked the question: "Peggy, if I really knew that I wanted to be with my partner, would I be going through this much discomfort?" In this case, she may not have known that she knew. That may sound like a mouthful, but think about that statement. You may not know that you know. Or the pain of knowing is too intense and your subconscious mind prevents you from opening your eyes (heart, soul, inner knowing) to the obvious. This client was holding on to a relationship hoping it would become something that it never was, and likely never would be, and she knew it.

Trust your instincts. If you have a knowing, it is because the energy is in the universe. Trust it. It reveals the truth.

We all need an education in the obvious.
Oliver Wendell Holmes

—⚜—

Knowing of possible future outcomes

There are unique individuals, sometimes described as clairvoyant, who are able to see the future in advance. If you do get a feeling or knowing about an event that may occur in the future, recognize that you have choices. You can examine your participation in the creation of this event and make new choices that can affect the outcome. In other words, if you get a bad feeling about something that is going to happen in the future, and you believe you can have a positive effect or influence the outcome, then use your creative energies and recreate the future outcome.

For example, if you have a feeling that you may be losing your job, then use your creative energy to personally deliver increased value to your employer, or alternatively, prepare yourself for another career opportunity or a career change.

You know more than you know. Believe this, and the conscious knowing will follow.

– 24 –

Gratitude

Gratitude unlocks the abundance of life.
Peggy McColl

—✦—

*S*everal years ago, I started the daily ritual of writing in a gratitude journal just before I retire at night. This simple exercise has
changed my life!

Why has it changed my life? My gratitude exercise has changed my life
because every day I notice the things, many things, that I am grateful
for. I did not notice these things before because I wasn't consciously
aware of the abundance and the many gifts that I have in my life.

This exercise has changed what I focus on. I now focus on the many
things that are great in my life, and I feel a sense of appreciation. Even
on the most challenging days, I find things in my life for which to be
grateful.

Many of us take our lives for granted. We often lose sight of the many
blessings in our life by comparing our own results with those of others who
appear to have more. We create our own dissatisfaction by comparison.

Earlier in the book, I shared with you part of Rico's story. Rico and I
also talked about gratitude and how being grateful has changed his life
considerably.

Rico shared with me that when he was a young boy his mother worked extremely hard, night and day, to provide for him and his brother. But, on occasion, he would go over to the neighbors' home and he would see that they had things that he didn't. Rico started to resent his mother and be angry with her for not buying these things for him. He would compare his life with that of his neighbors, who appeared to have more. Rico did not appreciate the things that he did have. He became selfish, and lost everything as a result.

Rico quickly learned when he was on the street that he had taken for granted all of the blessings he had had in his life. He didn't realize this until they were gone.

Now, he is a grateful man. He said the most important question that he asks himself is, "What am I most grateful for?" He finds that he answers with things that most people take for granted. He gives thanks for the smell of fresh clean sheets. He didn't have sheets when he lived in the street. He gives thanks for the clean clothes he has and the opportunity at Harvest House to help others and to contribute at a high level. Rico claims that his gratitude has attracted more great things into his life.

Gratitude is a state of being that will attract more to you because gratitude works with the natural laws of the universe. Whatever you focus your consistent thoughts on will expand.

Be grateful in advance. Give thanks for the things that you are about to receive. Genuinely show your appreciation to others. Express gratitude to others. You can do this with a simple smile or one flower, a kind word, or a written note.

Be grateful for all of your experiences. Be grateful for everything in your life. There is a blessing in everything. Within every adversity there is a seed of greatness.

The single most powerful "I am" statement that you can make is "I am grateful for..." Another way to phrase this most powerful statement is "Thank you, God, for..."

Be grateful for your health, your home, the electricity that lights the room, your friends, the fresh air you breathe, the rains that bring the flowers, the beauty of a sunset, the gift of choice and free will, a bubble bath, the birds that sing, the warmth of a burning fire in a fireplace, the change of seasons, the gift of a new day, the variety in music, the stars in the sky at night, the smell of a wonderful cologne, hearing the words "I love you," air conditioning on a hot humid day, waking up before the alarm, the hot water coming from the faucet, a smile, the ability to smile at another, a warm sweater, hair stylists, a good book and living in an abundant country...

Do not reject any part of your life, as it would be rejecting a part of yourself.

– 25 –

Journal Writing

Writing in journals is a way of recording your experiences. Having these journals allows you to return to the notes you have made about your experiences and contemplate those thoughts. This will give you clarity about your thought processes. You will be able to easily identify your beliefs and the filters through which you are viewing the world.

Keep journals of positive experiences and record how you felt at the time. This will help you later with building on positive states of being. We humans have a tendency to forget. Having a record allows you to go back and recall the event. If you write out all of the details, it will provide a greater perspective on the experience in order to help you really get in touch with the feelings. So, when you experience exhilaration, elation, unconditional love, extreme gratitude, or any other intense and positive emotion, record the details. Write out the thoughts you were having at the time, the words you were speaking, the expressions you had on your face, how you were feeling, what you were doing, how other people were reacting to you, and what changes you noticed at the time that were enlightening.

When you attend seminars, conferences and speaking engagements and you hear a great speaker, record the points that capture your attention. Write out the keys to higher thoughts and greater ideas. If you are feeling inspired, write out new goals and new dreams.

Carry a journal with you at all times. Record ideas, dreams and inspiring thoughts at the time that they come to your mind, and review them later while you are evaluating your goal lists.

Store the journals in a safe place. Keep copies of your goals in the journals. Write out your successes and victories as you experience them. If another has had a success and victory that you can relate to, write out how you felt. Write out what inspires you about other people who have accomplished great things.

When you review your journals, make new notes in your new journal about inspiring ideas that come to your mind. I once heard it said that "people who write in journals live their life twice." Reviewing great experiences, stories, victories, successes and wonderful events allows you to live them again in your mind and your body.

Most important, keep a gratitude journal and record in it every evening. It only takes thirty seconds to write down five things for which you are grateful.

You can use a small notebook or a desktop computer, notebook computer or Palm Pilot. The time investment in keeping a gratitude journal is minimal, and the rewards are immense.

– 26 –

Contribution

*B*e a giver. Look for ways that you can contribute to the lives of others. Become a contributor every day. Find ways to contribute to your employer, you customers, your children, your friends and family. When you are a contributor you will feel an incredible sense of satisfaction.

If you are in an enthusiastic and passionate state, share your enthusiasm with others. If you are strong in your state then you will have an impact on others. Enthusiasm is contagious. When you are spreading positive energy around, you are providing a source of energy for others.

If you are in business and you would like to experience greater success, then cause someone else to be successful, and thus experience success. Even if you are not feeling successful, put yourself in a successful state and be the source of success to another. This will make you feel successful.

Why does this work? It works because in order for you to give something to another, you must first have it. Therefore, if you were not being successful, you would not have been able to cause another to be successful. When we are being successful by bringing success to another, we are also opening up ourselves to receive success.

What is it that you would like to experience in your life—more prosperity, more patience, more love, recognition, praise, support? Give it away and cause another to experience these states of being.

Have you ever spoken words of praise to a child and watched them light up? You can send love to others without saying a word, just by being loving, with a smile, a warm hello or a helping hand. Love will be returned to you. It may not be returned immediately, but it will be returned.

Love is the magnet that attracts the best of everything.
Peggy McColl

– –

Ask people how you can help them. Ask others what their goals are and help them achieve their goals. This help may be something as simple as your advice, giving them a contact name or suggesting a book to read. Do things that help others reach their goals. Help unlock another person's unlimited potential and help them see their inner greatness.

Take the 24-hour challenge. Make a decision to be a totally loving person for a 24-hour period. Focus on this one state of being as an exercise, or choose another state if you wish. When you wake up in the morning immediately put yourself into a loving state. Everywhere you go throughout the day, give love. Be conscious about being loving. Say loving things. Do loving things. Notice how loving you are being with your thoughts, words and actions. If you notice that your thoughts shift to unloving thoughts, change them to loving thoughts. Then observe how you feel and notice the love that will be returned to you. The results will astound you.

– 27 –

Commitment and Dedication

Commitment

When you set a goal and commit yourself to this goal, you are making a promise to yourself to follow through. Being committed means demonstrating that you will do what you said you would do.

Focus follows commitment. Once you commit yourself to the goal, your focus will sustain the actions that follow.

Commitment is the conscious decision to make one choice and consciously not consider other choices. If you find yourself evaluating other chices after you have settled on a goal, then you are not completely committed to that goal.

How do you become committed? Just do it! Commitment is a decision. It is a natural result of knowing. You will know that you are committed because you are without other choices. The word *decision* comes from a Latin word that means to "cut off" all other possibilities.

Dedication

Dedication is an attachment to someone or something. It is also known as devotion or loyalty. When you are dedicated to your goal you will stick with it. When you are dedicated to a job, you demonstrate your dedication by your actions. It is the same with anything or anyone that you are dedicated to: you will remain true to them regardless of the circumstances.

Dedication is a component of goal achieving that will provide you with a more satisfying outcome because you will feel better about yourself. Whenever you give something of yourself to another that positively affects another, you feel better about yourself. When you exercise the state of being of *dedication* you become more familiar with the positive effects. The road to get to your goal will also be a more pleasurable trip for you if you have dedication. You will receive loyalty from others when they see your loyalty to them. And, just like human beings, your goals will be loyal to you and you will see the result of that when they manifest for you.

– 28 –

Honesty

*B*e honest with yourself. Being honest with yourself means listening to your innermost feelings and respecting the messages of those feelings. If you can't be truthful with yourself, you will not be truthful to another. If you are not being truthful to yourself, but you are trying to tell yourself that you are, or tell others that you are, then you will not be at peace; you will be not be at ease.

In my own life, there have been times when being honest with myself has led to immediate pain; however, denying the truth would have ultimately led to greater pain. In the interests of our own highest good, we may choose "short-term pain for long-term gain." At one point in my life I was in an unhealthy relationship. Even though the relationship had many wonderful highs, the knowing inside me clearly communicated that the conclusion of the relationship was imminent. It was painful to acknowledge the truth, but I knew that the truth was the doorway to new opportunities and renewed growth for both of us. The relationship did change form and we were no longer a couple; instead, we created a lasting and meaningful friendship.

Be honest with others. If you are not honest and truthful with others, people won't trust you, and trust is very important. If people begin to think that you are a dishonest person, they will give you less responsibility and not rely on you.

When you are not truthful, you can't feel good about yourself. Your self-confidence deteriorates. You will hurt others when you are not being truthful. Dishonesty creates a damaging ripple effect.

Tell the truth and the truth shall set you free. Never give up on truth, for truth never gives up on you.

– 29 –

Personal Mission Statement

As a man thinketh in his heart, so is he.
Proverbs 23:7

Personal Mission Statement is a declaration of what you believe to be your purpose in life. It is highly recommended that you keep your personal mission statement brief. You can say a lot with just a few words.

When your personal mission statement is completed, display it where you can see it every single day and read it out loud or silently to yourself. It will have a profound effect on your life.

Having a personal mission statement will cause you to perform better, handle challenges more effectively, and stay focused on your life purpose. Your level of happiness will increase because you are living a fulfilled life.

The following are some suggested guidelines for creating your personal mission statement:

- State it in the positive.
- Use action verbs such as "focused," "empower," "create," "be."

- Be able to experience it.
- Be relatively brief.
- Do not include universals such as "always," "never."
- Use inspiring, emotionally charged words.
- It should inspire you and make you proud.
- It represents the most important values.
- It demonstrates the contribution you will make.

The following is a sample of a personal mission statement:

The purpose of my life is to remember who I am, demonstrating the greatness within me every day, building on my strengths. To be grateful for the many gifts in my life and giving thanks. To be a world-renowned master in the field of personal, professional and corporate development, making a positive contribution to millions of lives all over the world.

A mission statement should be repeatable in order to be most powerful. A single sentence or a few words will suffice for most people. An example of a concise personal mission statement might be:

Change the face of the world for the better.

This mission statement could be expanded to say:

Change the face of the world for the better, one person at a time, one client at a time, one performance at a time.

– 30 –

Identity Board

*If you continue to **be** who you've always been,*
you'll continue to get what you've always got.
Peggy McColl

—⸎—

*I*dentity boards are designed to help *build the belief* about who you
are and to *remember* who you are. Once you have set your goals,
ask yourself, "Who do I need to become in order to achieve these
goals?" When you have made your list of states of being, then create an
identity board.

(Refer to the having/doing and being questions in Chapter 18 to assist
you with this exercise.)

This is how to create an identity board for yourself. Place a photograph of yourself in the middle of a piece of bristol board. Write on the
top of the board: "This is who I choose to be" or "Who am I?" Surround
your photograph with your states of being, as shown below.

What is the purpose of an identity board? The identity board reminds
you of the states of being in which you have chosen to engage. I place
my identity board directly beside my bed. At night just before I go to
sleep, and immediately following my gratitude journal entries, I stare at
my identity board. I then ask myself, "Is this who I was today? Did I

demonstrate these states of being?" In the morning when I awake, I look at my identity board again. This time I ask myself, "What am I committed to being today?" and then I say to myself "This is who I choose to be."

Sample of an identity board

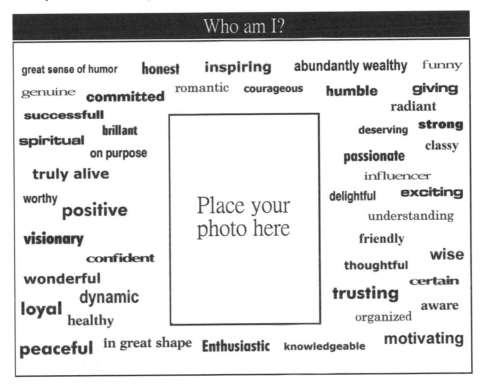

Who am I?

great sense of humor — **honest** — **inspiring** — **abundantly wealthy** — funny

genuine — **committed** — romantic — **courageous** — **humble** — **giving**

successfull — radiant

spiritual — **brillant** — deserving — **strong**

on purpose — **passionate** — classy

truly alive — influencer

worthy — **positive** — delightful — **exciting**

understanding

visionary — friendly

confident — thoughtful — **wise**

wonderful — certain

loyal — **dynamic** — **trusting** — aware

healthy — organized

peaceful — in great shape — **Enthusiastic** — knowledgeable — **motivating**

Place your photo here

– 31 –

In Summary

Happiness is not having what you want,
but wanting what you have.

—❧—

No doubt before you read this book you were already familiar with many or all of the great truths that are within its pages. But there are times when we need a gentle reminder of the things that we already know. As Oliver Wendell Holmes said, "We all need an education in the obvious." Not because we don't know, but simply because we have forgotten, and repetition is the key to mastery.

Therefore, please remember that you are a creative being and you have the ability to influence and/or create your outcomes. You are at choice always.

You are at choice as to what you will create in your life moving forward, where you will go, what you will experience, and how you will feel about the events in your life.

You are at choice as to what kind of a day you will have regardless of what shows up for you today. You are at choice as to whether you put this book down and say "great book," or you actually apply the valuable strategies that you have just learned, or make a list of the most important points that you have discovered. You are at choice as to whether you share the knowledge with your friends or loved ones.

As Nelson Mandela said so eloquently in his inaugural speech: "You are a child of God. Your playing small doesn't serve the world.... We were born to make manifest the glory of God that is within us. It's not just in some of us; it's in everyone."

There is true greatness within you and you have unlimited possibilities.

The following is a story of an individual demonstrating unlimited possibilities. This is the story of Mike Nemesvary.

In 1985, Mike Nemesvary, 24 years of age, was at the peak of his athletic career as a World Cup Champion freestyle skier. He had a phenomenal career in his sport, and had won numerous awards and competitions. He was a risk-taker and loved challenges.

Following a routine workout on his trampoline, Mike suffered an accident that led him to a new destiny. He lost his orientation to the ground and landed on his neck. The impact severed his spinal cord, leaving him a quadriplegic with minimal use of his arms.

Mike did not become defeated after his accident. He set new goals and has become an advocate for the disabled. He did not allow the accident to break his spirit.

Mike has recently completed a seven-month 'Round the World Challenge in an effort to raise money for spinal-cord research and rehabilitation. Traveling over 25,000 miles, passing through 4 continents, 18 countries and over 100 major cities, he is on track to raise $10 million and achieve the goal of raising the awareness of the abilities of people with disabilities and of the power of technology to help them realize their dreams.

When Mike was a teenager, did he have a conscious desire to complete a 'Round the World Challenge? No. His dream was to be a world freestyle ski champion. He achieved that dream and had begun to focus on new, related goals. But, on one fateful day, he was faced with new choices. This event led Mike to ask himself possibility questions like: What do I do now? What will I accomplish now with my life that will make a difference?

Mike's physical body may have changed, but his identity did not. He did not allow his identity to change because part of his physical body was no longer being used. Inside he was a champion, on the slopes and off. He understands that when you accept the challenges, you can enjoy the exhilaration of the victory.

He demonstrates the power of attitude, will, drive, determination, commitment and perseverance. When Mike was competing in his sport he was continually faced with challenges. The emotional muscles that he built early in his career now support him in his new career. He is prepared to handle adversity and overcome challenges.

Now Mike is making a positive difference in the lives of others. He is a man with a purpose and a cause. Mike knows how to set goals and he knows how to reach them. Mike is traveling the world, raising money and awareness for an extremely worthy cause, and at the same time, he is being an example of true possibility to everyone who has the privilege of meeting him.

Today is a brand new day. Go forward with renewed faith and excitement and expect great things. Become all that you can be. Be the captain of your destiny. Know that you are an incredible being.

Have faith in the universal power of creation. This power is within you waiting to be expressed.

Choose to create your own destiny rather than living your life in a reactive state. You have that gift. True freedom is not the freedom to follow every thought that comes into your mind, but to take your future into your own hands.

On Being is about living your life with awareness and choice, and having the confidence to commit to your path. Take control of your life today and create an extraordinary future for you and for those you love.

All the happiness you will ever find lies within you.
Peggy McColl

Please share your success stories with me so that I can share them with others. Write about the benefits, contributions and learning experiences that you have realized as a result of applying the ideas, tools and/or strategies in this book and I will, in turn, share them with the world. Your stories will be the source of inspiration and faith for others. Thank you for the privilege and the opportunity to share a lifetime of experiential learning. Please send your stories by e-mail to stories@OnBeing.com.

SECTION 5

References

This section is designed to summarize the tools and techniques outlined in the book. Use this section for reference.

Support Questions

Finding Your Passion
What do I really want to do with my life?
What am I passionate about?
What do I love?
Where would I go if I had the freedom to go anywhere?
What would I do if I could do anything?
What would I have if there were no limits?
Who would I become?
What gives me the most satisfaction in my life?
What do I really enjoy doing in my spare time?
What motivates me?

What inspires me?

What excites me?

What drives me?

When I have had the experience of jumping out of bed with excitement, what was the cause?

What have I done in the past that has given me the most pleasure?

How do I want to contribute to the lives of others?

What would I like to give to others?

How would I like to be remembered?

If I granted you one wish, and you knew that that wish would be granted, what would you wish for?

Goal Setting and Decision Making

What do I really want to accomplish?

Who do I really want to be (become)?

What skills do I want to master?

What do I really want to have?

What do I want to be recognized for?

How do I want my family/friends/partner/customers to feel about me?

What would I do if I knew that I could not fail?

What are the targets I want to achieve (financially, in revenue, net worth)?

What would I like to experience in my life?

What do I choose to experience in my life?

What do I want to have, do or be?

What decisions do I need to make today toward the achievement of my goals?

What choices will I make today toward the attainment of my goals?

Goal Setting and Focus

What actions will I take today that will take me in the direction of my goals?

Where do I choose to focus my consistent thoughts?
What will I visualize today that supports my goals?
How will I increase my level of focus?
What disciplines will I now engage in that will help support me in the achievement of my goals?

Having/Doing and Being

In order to have a loving and fulfilling relationship in my life, what do I need to be?
In order to have a successful career, what do I need to be?
In order to have financial abundance, what do I need to be?
In order to be recognized as the best in my chosen field, what do I need to be?
In order to have great grades in school, what do I need to be?
In order to have increased sales, what do I need to be?
In order to know that I am contributing at the highest level, what do I need to be?
In order to have a well toned and healthy body, what do I need to be?
In order to have balance in my life, what do I need to be?
In order to be an outstanding parent, what do I need to be?
In order to have wonderful and meaningful friends, what do I need to be?
In order to have a luxurious and opulent lifestyle, what do I need to be?
In order to have peace with who I am, what do I need to be?
In order to live my life on purpose, what do I need to be?

Handling Adversity and Overcoming Challenges

What is great about this?
What would a loving person do now?
What else could this mean (answer in a positive way)?
What will I remember about this event that will help me in the future?

What can I do right now to make this better?

What will I focus on right now to help me feel better about this?

How can I use this to benefit myself and others?

What is the blessing in this?

Being

Is this who I choose to be?

Who am I?

Is this who I am?

What can I be for you?

What will I do now to demonstrate the highest level of my states of being?

As I am an unconditionally loving being, what will I do now?

How can I demonstrate the highest aspect of who I am?

How will I give to others to make a positive difference in the life of another?

How will I help others achieve their goals?

What am I committed to being today that will take me in the direction of my goals?

How will I demonstrate my highest level of being loving right now?

What kind of day would I like to experience today? What do I need to be in order to have that kind of day?

For what am I most grateful?

How will I make this day a masterpiece?

Monitoring Your Progress and Noticing the Results

Did I break down the goal into baby steps or smaller goals and create stepping stones to reach the larger goal?

Am I missing something that is obvious and I haven't taken the time to reflect or evaluate the action steps that I am taking?

Am I taking the wrong route? Is there a better way?

Have I considered all of the options?

Should I consider changing directions or try another approach?

Have I been watching all the signs along the way?

Have I been returning to old conditioning and moving backward instead of forward?

Have I created a plan that is solid enough? Or do I need to review my plan and make changes?

Am I taking the long road; is there a better route?

Am I totally off track?

What resources can I use to help me with achieving this goal?

Who can help me achieve this goal?

What tools will I use to help me achieve this goal?

Is this taking me in the direction of my goal or farther away?

What do I now need to do (be) in order to reach my desired result?

How will I know if I am getting the right results? (This question will allow you to anticipate the results in advance.)

Beingness Guide

If you are experiencing this state of being:	This is a possible cause:	This is a suggestion to enable a new state of being:	These are the states of being to engage in:
Anger, resentment	You are being fearful and afraid of something. You may be afraid to let go of the anger, fearing it will cause you pain.	Relax your mind and body. Breathe deeply. Get in touch with the root cause of your anger. Make a decision to stop the anger and/or the resentment as it is detrimental to you and others.	Be loving Be forgiving Be calm
Sadness, depression	Limited beliefs. You have closed yourself off from being loving (accepting or giving). You are focusing on the negative only and repeating old patterns. You are looking at the lack in your life.	Think of what is great in your life. Do a gratitude exercise. Be loving to yourself and to another. Create new rituals (patterns of behavior) to empower the new states of being.	Be grateful Be appreciative Be happy

If you are experienc-ing this state of being:	This is a possible cause:	This is a suggestion to enable a new state of being:	These are the states of being to engage in:
Tension, impatience	You are narrowing your focus and limiting your thoughts of possibility.	Relax your body. Take deep breaths. Become still and quietly listen. Put yourself into a state of faith.	Be patient Be faithful Be trusting Be relaxed
Dissatisfaction	You are no longer enjoying your present condition. You are not appreciating the great things in your life.	You are at choice always. If you are dis-satisfied, get excited, because you have the opportunity to change it or change how you feel about it. Make a decision and take action.	Be excited Be grateful

If you are experiencing this state of being:	This is a possible cause:	This is a suggestion to enable a new state of being:	These are the states of being to engage in:
Worry, stress	You have lost faith. You may have forgotten that you have the ability to choose.	There is no sense in worrying about the things that you have control over because you have control over them. There is no sense in worrying about the things that you do not have any control over because you don't have any control over them.	Be peaceful Be relaxed Be confident
Hostility	Your anger may be out of control. You have deep-rooted emotions that you have not dealt with.	Get to the root cause of your hostility. Seek professional help, if required.	Be gentle

If you are experiencing this state of being:	This is a possible cause:	This is a suggestion to enable a new state of being:	These are the states of being to engage in:
Distrust	You are not being honest with yourself and with others. Or, you have created false beliefs. Or, your inner voice is sending you a warning and you need to listen.	Become honest with yourself and your innermost feelings. Communicate how you truly feel to others in a loving way.	Be trusting Be honest Be loving
Doubt, uncertainty	You have lost faith in yourself, in others and in the Universal Energy.	Replace doubt with faith. Write a list of reasons why you can be faithful now.	Be faithful Be certain

If you are experiencing this state of being:	This is a possible cause:	This is a suggestion to enable a new state of being:	These are the states of being to engage in:
Extreme hurt	You are possibly feeling insecure or inadequate or your self-esteem is low.	Ask yourself: "What else could this situation mean?" (only answer with positive answers)	Be loving to yourself Be confident
Lost, helpless	You are simply forgetting who you are and what your capabilities are. You are never lost; you are just not remembering. You have an abundance of opportunities and unlimited personal power.	Remember that you are an incredible person with unlimited potential and possibilities. Everything you need is within you now.	Be on purpose Be aware

If you are experiencing this state of being:	This is a possible cause:	This is a suggestion to enable a new state of being:	These are the states of being to engage in:
Unworthy, undeserving	You are allowing another's negative influence to be accepted into your mind. Your beliefs about who you really are, are inaccurate.	You are a child of God and your natural state is worthiness. Love yourself first.	Be deserving Be worthy Be totally loving
Discouraged	You are allowing negativity in. Look at what this feeling is revealing to you. Is it giving you a clear message to review your decisions? Or are you simply losing faith?	Evaluate the source of the feeling. Get excited about the opportunity this offers, or create new exciting opportunities. You have choices. Regain your faith in yourself and your ability and in the Universe.	Be excited Be faithful

If you are experiencing this state of being:	This is a possible cause:	This is a suggestion to enable a new state of being:	These are the states of being to engage in:
Guilty	You are behaving in a manner that is in direct opposition to your values.	If you have done something that is, in your opinion, wrong, then correct it. Make it right. Forgive yourself and make a decision to learn from the experience, and move on.	Be loving
Mean, cruel, nasty	You are hurting. You are not loving yourself. You have hurt yourself and are hurting yourself more by being in these states, or you are allowing another's actions to hurt you, which is detrimental to you.	Stop hurting others, as it hurts you too. Love yourself. Give love away.	Be kind Be considerate Be thoughtful Be loving

If you are experiencing this state of being:	This is a possible cause:	This is a suggestion to enable a new state of being:	These are the states of being to engage in:
Insecure	You are doing things or have done things that diminish your own self-worth. Or, you may have hurt someone.	Love yourself and love all others. List the things that are great about you: your strengths, your strongest characteristics; your accomplishments and achievements. Set new goals and create plans for the achievement and get on with the work.	Be confident Be loving
Nervous	Relax. You are likely not breathing. You are focusing on fear-based thinking.	Turn your nervousness into positive energy.	Be relaxed

If you are experiencing this state of being:	This is a possible cause:	This is a suggestion to enable a new state of being:	These are the states of being to engage in:
Unmotivated	You don't have any goals or you are doing nothing toward achieving the goals that you do have.	Set some goals, or take action toward the attainment of your goals. Write out the benefits you will realize when you do achieve your goals.	Be focused Be excited Be motivated
Fearful	You have lost faith. You are focused on loss or lack.	Think of positive possibilities. Take action.	Be faithful Be courageous
Lonely	You have shut yourself off from receiving.	Find someone else who is lonely and help them feel loved and wanted.	Be loving Be giving Be warm

If you are experienc-ing this state of being:	This is a possible cause:	This is a suggestion to enable a new state of being:	These are the states of being to engage in:
Unattractive	You are looking at the negative only.	Beauty comes from within. Beauty too is vibration. Do something to make yourself look better. See an image expert. Take great care of yourself.	Be beautiful
Drained	You are allowing out-side influences or nega-tivity to drag you down.	Focus on the great things in your life and your opportunities. Get the rest that you need and take care of your body.	Be refreshed Be energetic

Monthly Activities for Goal Achieving

- Set monthly goals as stepping stones to reach your larger goals.
- Measure and monitor your progress.
- Measure and monitor your states of being.
- Practice engaging in the states of being that support your goals. Be the source of these states to others.
- Create a plan to achieve your goals.
- Follow the plan you have set for your goal achieving.
- Create a contingency plan or backup plan.
- If your results are not the results that you desire, try something else.
- Enter action items into your daily schedule or time management system.
- Visualize yourself already in possession of your goals.
- Feel what it will feel like when you achieve your goals.
- Decide how you will celebrate when you achieve your goals.
- Establish your daily code of conduct (disciplines) and follow it.
- Stay focused on your goals in everything that you do.
- Ask yourself empowering questions.
- Keep an Accomplishment file and enter the goals once you achieve them. Add thank you cards and your favorite sayings. Review this file from time to time.
- Be grateful for the gifts in your life and the gifts that you are creating.
- Acknowledge others for the gifts that they bring to your life.

References

Summary of Quotations in *On Being...The Creator of Your Destiny*

For every disciplined effort there is a multiple reward.
Jim Rohn

Whatever the mind of man can conceive and believe it can achieve.
Napoleon Hill

People are anxious to improve their circumstances, but unwilling to improve themselves. They therefore remain bound.
James Allen

To dream anything that you want to dream; that is the beauty of the human mind. To do anything that you want to do; that is the strength of the human will. To trust yourself to test your limits; that is the courage to succeed.
Bernard Edmonds

You can have anything you want—if you want it badly enough. You can be anything you want to be, do anything you set out to accomplish, if you hold to that desire with singleness of purpose.
Abraham Lincoln

Faith without works is dead.
James 2:20

Being is energy vibrating at the highest level.
Peggy McColl

[People] do not attract that which they want, but that which they are.
James Allen

*A blizzard creates the right conditions so a person
can build shelter from it.*
John Amagoalik

*You are at choice always, in all ways.
Enthusiasm is at the bottom of all progress. With it there is
accomplishment. Without it, there are only alibis.*
Walter Chrysler

*The greatest discovery is that human beings can alter their
lives by altering their attitudes of mind.*
William James

*Now faith is the substance of things hoped for,
the evidence of things not seen.*
Hebrews 11:1

*If one advances confidently in the direction of their dreams, and
endeavors to live a life which they have imagined, they will meet
with a success unexpected in common hours.*
Henry David Thoreau

*If you have no confidence in self, you are twice defeated in the race
of life. With confidence, you have won even before you have started.*
Marcus Garvey

We all need an education in the obvious.
Oliver Wendell Holmes

Gratitude unlocks the abundance of life.
Peggy McColl

Love is the magnet that attracts the best of everything.
Peggy McColl

As a man thinketh in his heart, so is he.
Proverbs 23:7

If you continue to be who you've always been,
you'll continue to get what you've always got.
Peggy McColl

Happiness is not having what you want, but wanting what you have.
All the happiness you will ever find lies within you.
Peggy McColl

Goal Chart (Sample)

For an example of a completed goal chart, please see page 120.

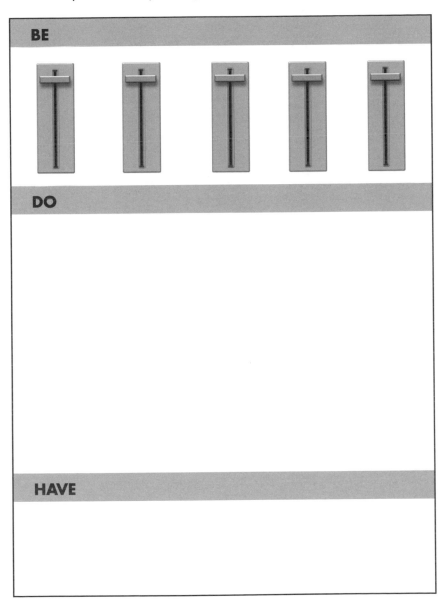

Recommended Readings

A Return to Love, Marianne Williamson
Acres of Diamonds, Russell H. Conwell
As a Man Thinketh, James Allen
Awaken the Giant Within, Anthony Robbins
Chicken Soup for the Soul®, Jack Canfield and Mark Victor Hansen
Communion with God, Neale Donald Walsch
Conversations with God, Book 1, Book 2 & Book 3 , Neale Donald Walsch
Creating Affluence, Deepak Chopra, M.D.
Do What You Love, the Money Will Follow, Marsha Sinetar
Feel the Fear and Do It Anyway, Susan Jeffers, Ph.D.
Friendship with God, Neale Donald Walsch
The Greatest Salesman in the World, Og Mandino
Grow Younger, Live Longer, Deepak Chopra, M.D., and David Simon, M.D.
How to Stop Worrying and Start Living, Dale Carnegie
How to Think Like a Millionaire, Mark Fisher
If You Could See What I Hear, Kathy Buckley
I'm OK, You're OK, Thomas A. Harris, M.D.
The Language of Letting Go, Melody Beattie
Living, Loving & Learning, Leo Buscaglia, Ph.D.
Love Is Letting Go of Fear, Gerald G. Jampolsky, M.D.
The Magic of Believing, Claude M. Bristol
Manifest Your Destiny, Dr. Wayne Dyer
Moments of Grace, Neale Donald Walsch
The Monk Who Sold His Ferrari, Robin S. Sharma
The Path to Love, Deepak Chopra, M.D.
The Power Is Within You, Louise Hay
The Power of Positive Thinking, Norman Vincent Peale
The Power of Your Subconscious Mind, Dr. Joseph Murphy
Psycho-Cybernetics, Dr. Maxwell Maltz
The Richest Man in Babylon, George S. Clason

References

The Science of Getting Rich, Wallace D. Wattles

The Seat of the Soul, Gary Zukav

The Self-Talk Solution, Dr. Shad Helmstetter

The 7 Habits of Highly Effective People, Stephen R. Covey

7 Strategies for Wealth & Happiness, Jim Rohn

Success Is a Choice , Rick Pitino

Think and Grow Rich, Napoleon Hill

Unlimited Power, Anthony Robbins

Unstoppable, Cynthia Hersey

What to Say When You Talk to Yourself, Dr. Shad Helmstetter

What You Think of Me Is None of My Business, Terry Cole-Whittaker

Winning Every Day, Lou Holtz

You Can Heal Your Life, Louise Hay

Your Erroneous Zones, Dr. Wayne Dyer

Your Infinite Power to Be Rich, Dr. Joseph Murphy

Your Invisible Power, Genevieve Behrend

Coming Soon
Test Your Current States of Being...*Online*

Beginning in Spring 2002, you can test your current states of being at the On Being website www.OnBeing.com !

Log on to the On Being website, enter the States of Being Testing area, enter the relevant information, and go through a timed sequence of questions to determine your dominant states of being.

Find out if you are, in fact, being loving, being grateful, being patient, et cetera. You will also find suggestions on how to put yourself into specific states of being.

If you would like to be notified via e-mail of the launch date, please send your e-mail address to info@OnBeing.com

The Destiny Foundation

A portion of every dollar earned in profit from the sale of this book is donated to the Destiny Foundation.

The Destiny Foundation is a non-profit organization focused on supporting children's charities and children's personal development programs.

For more information please call (613) 299-5722 or contact info@OnBeing.com.

About the *Author*
Peggy McColl

Peggy McColl has been a featured speaker throughout Canada and the United States. Whether as a keynote conference speaker or booked for a corporate semianr, Peggy combines a depth of knowledge of her material with an unparalleled level of enthusiasm.

Peggy works closely with the client to ensure that the material delivered is both relevant and topical. The hard hitting themes are delivered in a humorous and animated fashion so that the concepts are truly understood and remembered.

Peggy delivers customized keynote speeches and presentations on the following topics:

Achieving Organizational Success

Based on Peggy's groundbreaking work on Goal Management Achievement Planning System **(GoalMAPS)**, this speech will motivate even the most experienced senior executive. Designed for both public and private sector organizations, Achieving Organizational Success provides the blueprint for prioritizing goals and objectives in such a way that every segment of the organization works together to contribute to their success.

Be The Source

Unlock your hidden potential by releasing all of your creative energy. Peggy unveils innovative strategies to unleash the power within so that each of us can turn our desires into reality.

The Dynamics of Leading a Winning Team

Learn the tips of leading your organization with integrity while motivating and empowering your team to succeed. Peggy's practical advice will result in immediate dividends for any organization that strives to achieve their objectives.

Create Your Ultimate Destiny

Based on Peggy McColl's book *On Being...The Creator of Your Destiny*, this speech focuses on formalizing our personal desires for a successful future. Following the blueprint established by the Professional Outcome Goal System (POGS), Peggy enthralls and motivates her audience to take responsibility for their actions and proactively create the future they want for themselves.

Peggy McColl has devoted much of her professional life to working closely with individuals and high-level professionals, assisting them to reach their maximum potential. In addition, she has provided the framework to help growing companies and organizations reach their goals.

Peggy is an acknowledged expert in goal achievement systems. As the founder and current president & CEO of Dynamic Destinies Inc., Peggy is the driving force behind the development of the Goal Management Achievement Planning System (GoalMAPS). This program is the most compelling and strategic goal system of its kind.

Peggy has worked with a variety of high-profile national and international organizations, including Bell, Jaguar, Shell, Ericsson, the Department of National Defence and a number of Olympic teams.

During her career, Peggy has studied and trained with world-renowned experts, including Dr. Deepak Chopra, Mark Victor Hansen, Dr. Napoleon Hill, Sir John Templeton, Brian Tracey, Ken Blanchard and Anthony Robbins.

Prior to founding Dynamic Destinies, Peggy had more than 20 years of senior level management experience in the high technology industry.

Peggy lives in Ottawa, Canada, with her son Michel.

Here's how to contact Peggy:

peggy@destinies.com   **www.destinies.com**

Dynamic Destinies Inc.

1 Stafford Road, Suite 312, Nepean, Ontario, Canada K2H 1B9

(613) 299-5722 in Ottawa

or toll-free at 1-866-OnBeing (1-866-662-3464)

Tools for Success—Order Yours Today!

We hope you have enjoyed
On Being...The Creator of Your Destiny

To order additional copies of *On Being...The Creator of Your Destiny* by Peggy McColl, please contact Destinies Publishing at 1-866-OnBeing (1-866-662-3464) toll free or 1-613-299-5722 or visit our website at www.onbeing.com

Peggy is truly a dynamo. She lives, breathes and experiences all that she teaches. If you want to change your life, change your being. Peggy's book will set you on the course to take control of your own destiny.
Paul Montelongo, author of *101 Power Strategies*

Now Available!
The *You Can Create Your Ultimate Destiny* Workbook

Based on the proven success methods found in the phenomenal book *On Being...The Creator of Your Destiny,* the You Can Create Your Ultimate Destiny Workbook is a step-by-step guide to empower you to achieve all of your goals.

You will learn how to:
- Take control of your life
- Harness the power within you
- Set life-affirming goals
- Create an action plan to succeed
- Eliminate self destructive behaviors
- Choose your own destiny
- Commit yourself to success
- Create an environment filled with confidence
- Life a life full of abundance

This workbook is designed with step-by-step exercises and easy to apply tools to take your life to a higher level of satisfaction and achievement.

Being Switches (Single Panel)
The Being Switches are one of the powerful and simple methods of measuring your most empowering states of being for goal achievement, as described in this book. Discover if you are truly being committed, honest, loving, professional, successful, et cetera? And, at what level are you being this? This clarity will give you the power to increase your focus and effectively maintain the necessary states of being in order to easily achieve your goals.

Being Switch (Multi-panel)
Focus on the dominant states of being required to achieve a specific goal by investing in the multi-panel Being Switch.

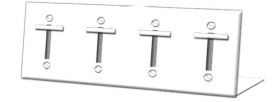

Future books to be released by Peggy McColl

On Being...A Successful Organization

On Being...The Creator of Your Destiny: True Success Stories